My Cancer Has Many Faces

Alero Dabor

© 2014 Alero Dabor. All rights reserved.

Cover art by fiverr.com/capooter

Edited by Therese Arkenberg

ISBN: 978-1-326-03299-9

Thank you for purchasing this book. This book is the copyrighted property of the author and may not be reproduced or distributed for any commercial use. Limited non-commercial reproduction and sharing, including the use of quotes and excerpts in reviews, is welcomed. Your support of this author is greatly appreciated!

TABLE OF CONTENTS

Dedication	*4*
Foreword	*7*
Phase One: Diagnosis	*11*
Phase Two: Treatment	*72*
Phase Three: Survival	*129*
Epilogue	*144*
Appendix 1: Ayulie's Story	*155*
Appendix 2: Junior's Story	*156*
Appendix 3: Demi's Story	*159*
Appendix 4: Risi's Story	*163*
Appendix 5: Foster's Story	*166*

***

My cancer journey is based on the experience of a single parent. The fact that I happened to be single, and to have a family, was not in the least irrelevant when I received my cancer diagnosis.

Yet cancer does not discriminate. It does not care who you are rich, poor, married, single, divorced, happy sad, young, old, fat or thin. It really does not care about your feelings.

Cancer has many faces. It is not only a physical disease, but also a disease that gets to you financially, emotionally and spiritually. It can be a lonely disease.

Cancer takes a life of its own and has a life of its own

Because cancer has many faces, it is also a disease that enables you to become empowered, overcome fear, live life to the fullest, reinvent yourself and thank Him for your life.

You can take control of your cancer. This is something cancer teaches you if you decide to take ownership of your journey. Embrace your power to choose, love it and work with it in your body, in your mind and in your soul.

Cancer could be the best thing that may have happened to you or it could be the worst thing that ever happened to you.

That decision will always be yours, as you learn to live and love your experiences, even through cancer.

This book grew from a set of journal entries I wrote over the course of my cancer, from July 2006 when I first had a hint that all was not well, through the discovery of what I then referred to as 'my ailment,' through treatment until the spring of 2007, when I began to redefine myself from cancer sufferer to cancer survivor. I hope that reading it sheds light on my experience and offers my perspective for you, dear reader, to consider. We may not agree on all things, and that is all right. As I have thought before, if my story reaches just one person, that will be enough.

This book is dedicated:

To my dear son Ayulie, for without you, I would not be alive today to write to tell the story of a single mother who became a cancer sufferer to become a survivor. For that I thank you.

To my son Jnr. For one so young, you showed so much maturity as a caregiver.

To my niece, Demi, who is simply the best. For one so young, you have much wisdom.

To my sister, Thelma, for all your help, laughter and understanding.

To my mother.

To my brothers.

To Auntie Roli and Uncle Godfrey, for all the trips to the hospital.

To all my friends and family for being there for me.

This book is also for any mother, sister, brother, friend, spouse, partner, or colleague who has had a cancer diagnosis. It is also a book for those caring for anyone with cancer.

The book is for anyone and everyone.

It tells the story of a single mother who, several years ago, was diagnosed with cancer. You will feel her pain, know her lamentations, her tears, her confusion and her anguish. What is more important, you will be able to feel her strength, her courage, her resilience and her determination to get through this period. You will know her joy, her laughter and her humour.

The book will tell you of how she went from being a cancer sufferer to becoming a cancer survivor. How she has chosen to reinvent herself with new dreams, goals and aspirations while she continues to live with cancer.

She is a real person: a mother, a sister, a friend a daughter and a colleague.

The truth is that if you survive cancer, there is life after it, despite the challenges you face along the way.

Foreword

'Cancer can be a lonely disease,' Alero writes in the opening paragraphs of her book. The story that unfolds over subsequent pages lays bare cancer's invasion of every part of her life: the physical, financial, emotional and spiritual consequences of her diagnosis and of the treatment she received—and also, somewhat controversially, refused. It is a heroic tale, told with Alero's characteristic humour and humility.

Alero knows that everybody's cancer story is different, and that each individual will have their own way of managing it, adjusting to it, dealing with it or even ignoring it, as the case may be. She makes no assumptions that others will approach their illness in a similar way to her, but she presents some universal truths that will resonate with anyone who has had personal experience of cancer: the contradictory emotions, the unpredictable moods, the anguish of making big decisions in the midst of uncertainty ('Do I take this wonderful job that has come at exactly the wrong time, or don't I?'). She vividly describes the joy of things often taken for granted: a good night's sleep, the kindness of friends, the unstinting support of family, the renewed enjoyment of the beauty of a familiar city, walks in the park.

An encounter with cancer does not end at the point that the doctors say, 'You have recovered; we don't need to see you again.' Alero continues her story through the hidden difficulties of making a new life after cancer: 'Being diagnosed with cancer and going through treatment was actually the easy part; the hardest part for me is survivorship.' Coping with cancer's often invisible after-effects can last years beyond treatment, including managing the expectations of others that having been given the 'all clear' one is back to full strength, and one's own expectations of being able to carry on with life as it was before. Alero shows how 'cancer changes one without our realizing it,' and that it is not a straightforward matter to make sense of a different body, changed priorities, and a new-and-yet-the-same self.

In the years following her illness, Alero has used the knowledge she has gained and her talent for building relationships with people to become a 'voice' for others going through the same ordeal, contributing a survivor's perspective on service and policy developments. And it was in this role that I met Alero for the first time. She was one of about fifteen people—mainly cancer health care professionals, researchers, service managers and policy makers—meeting to decide on an evaluation strategy for a project we were all involved with, designed to support people with cancer to return to work. We were assembled around a rather soulless boardroom table with our corrugated cardboard cups of coffee, discussing the relative merits of various outcome measures and statistical approaches. Alero sat listening intently and as we got no closer to reaching a consensus, she spoke. 'I think,' she said, 'that you have all lost sight of what really matters to the people you are trying to help—people with cancer. The thing that mattered most to me was that I felt listened to and respected. That I was treated like a human being who could make her own decisions, even when—in fact, especially when—those decisions were not the ones that health professionals thought were the right ones. I wanted to know that I had the right information and support to make the best possible choices for my life and my family.'

My work involves finding ways to support people living with and beyond cancer to remain in or return to employment, where that is their wish. It's an area where there are lots of different stakeholders: NHS cancer services, the Department of Work and Pensions, employers, rehabilitation service providers, policy organisations, charitable funders–each with their own idea of what constitutes a good outcome. The NHS, for example, wants to save money on long-term follow up, whereas the DWP is concerned with keeping people in work and off benefits. Rehabilitation services, on the other hand, want to ensure that they secure the resources they need to meet people's work-related needs. In the clamour, it's easy for the patient's voice to be drowned out. Alero works hard to make sure this doesn't happen.

Over the past four years, Alero's unswerving support for me and for the work that I do has been invaluable. I hold on to a remark that she made a while ago, over lunch at MacDonald's in London's Victoria Station, at a time when bureaucratic and administrative complications with a study I was working on felt overwhelming: 'Your research matters, Gail. It will change people's lives.' She makes it impossible to give up.

Gail Eva
London
October 2014

PHASE ONE: DIAGNOSIS

28 July, 2006

It all began on a classically beautiful summer's day. The sun was shining, the sky was blue, the birds were singing. Life was looking good and I was feeling much better. I had been extremely fatigued the past several months. Every morning, Monday–Friday, I had a normal routine: wake up at 5:00 a.m., get ready for work, ensure Ayulie got up, had breakfast, and was ready for school. Once he was off, I would drive to work. This took me between 45 minutes and an hour, subject to traffic. While I currently worked as a Leasehold Services Manager, I had always dreamt of becoming a practicing Property Solicitor. After working nine to five, on Tuesday, Wednesday, and Thursday I would go the BPP College of Law at Holborn straight from the office. College went from 6–9 p.m., so that I would get home just before midnight on the three evenings I attended.

It was a lifestyle I had become accustomed to. I had obtained my Law degrees—that is, my LLB and my Masters of Law—while working full time and studying part-time, with absolutely no problems whatsoever. To all intents and purposes, the Legal Practice Course I now embarked on was just another class.

However, during one of my lectures in March 2006 I realized my concentration was shattered. I wasn't taking anything in. The course that seemed relatively straightforward to most of the students felt beyond my understanding. I still vividly remember how I struggled to get to grips with Intellectual Property and Commerce.

In addition to feeling tired during my lectures, even on days I did not go to college I went right to bed when I got home. Skipping dinner, I would sleep from 7:00 p.m. until I woke the next morning at 5:00 a.m.

During weekends, I would sleep literally all day. In hindsight, this fatigue I experienced was not normal. There was something indeed odd about how I was constantly tired, with no relief. Exhaustion never went away, no matter how long I slept. Yet at the time I ignored it, and put my tiredness down to a very busy schedule.

When the summer holiday came, and I had no college to go to after work, I could come home, sleep and spend time with Ayulie. I just began to feel better. I was more relaxed, as all I had to do was go to work. Yet the truth is, I was not well at all.

It has always been a balancing act to spend quality time with my son while working full time and studying part time. During the summer holiday, I was able to take the day off. Having this day with my fourteen-year-old Ayulie and doing things with him was always something I cherished. Today was no exception. We woke up early and decided to go into central London, taking in the atmosphere. We went window shopping on Oxford Street, looking for nothing in particular.

We got home around 6:00 p.m. My son was being ever so helpful around the house. Ayulie is usually a lovely child, but has never particularly enjoyed doing his chores. Not many young people do. However, on this particular day he actually volunteered to do them. That got me wondering— *This is not like him! Hmm, what's up?*

I asked if he wanted anything. Perhaps he was seeking a reward for offering to do some chores. At my question, Ayulie started crying. He told me that he had a dream that his maths teacher had called him out of the classroom to tell him I had been involved in car crash and had not survived.

He had tears pouring down his face. I told him not to cry, as it was only a dream. He could obviously see that I was whole and hearty and there was nothing to worry about.

The dream on its own might not amount to much, but what happened afterwards makes it stranger than fiction.

I went to my bedroom to change that evening and for no apparent reason, I decided to do a breast examination. To this day I do not know why I did the examination—perhaps it was because of my son's dream, but why that pointed to my breasts I cannot guess. I could not remember the last time I did a breast examination. It was July, so there probably hadn't been something on the television to raise cancer breast awareness like there is each October. However, this night I did it. And I felt a lump on the right side of my breast.

Hey! Whatever my reasons for doing the examination there was a lump, simple and plain as that. But I felt no real alarm, at least not yet.

I said nothing to Ayulie; there was nothing to say. He was young, and I didn't want to bring the issue up with him, and I didn't really know any more than he did what was going on. Cancer had never been mentioned in our household.

My son and I stayed up that night to about 10:00 p.m. watching television together. When we finally went to bed, I checked again. The lump was still there, but I decided there was nothing I could do about it. I finally drifted off to sleep.

Saturday, 29 July

This was another beautiful summer day. I woke up wondering what the lump was about. As I went about my morning routine, I checked and it was still there.

I decided to go my GP, who opened on Saturday mornings for a couple of hours for booked appointments and emergencies only. It was not a walk-in system on Saturday's.

I told the receptionist that I would like to see the GP. She asked me what for, and I told her I had a lump on the right side of my breast.

She allowed me to see the GP.

Apparently this counted as an emergency.

Yet after examining me, my GP said it was a cyst and that I had nothing to worry about. I left the surgery and carried on with my daily activities.

But there was something I didn't know at the time. Without me even suspecting, my GP wrote a letter to the Princess Royal in Orpington asking for me to be seen in the breast cancer clinic whenever possible.

Before that, I was not in the least bit worried or perturbed. I knew there was nothing wrong with me, so why would I worry? Prayer was enough to see me through. Aside from my fatigue and this strange lump, life went back to business as usual.

30 July

By the time my birthday rolled around on 30 July, I had forgotten about the lump and was carrying on according to normal. No fuss, no worries. For some reason, I did not do anything in particular to celebrate my birthday. It was very quiet, just Ayulie and I. This was how I wanted it. Despite everything else that happened around it, despite the fact that it could have been my last, it was not a memorable birthday.

10 August

As I said, my GP had written to the Breast Cancer Clinic at Princess Royal in Orpington. I had been given an appointment for today, 10 August.

I went to the hospital with Ayulie and my niece, Demi, because it was the summer holiday and I was looking after both of them that day.

Our drive to the hospital was pleasant. I registered my attendance and waited for my turn to be seen by the consultant, Mr Singh. He examined me and said that it was only a cyst, but to be on the safe side I should go for a mammogram.

I was far from pleased. I thought the GP was making a fuss over nothing. I didn't understand why he had written to the Breast Cancer clinic for a cyst. I wasn't worried, though, because cysts are generally common, and they don't pose any serious health issues. I just waited for the fuss and examinations to be over.

So I had come to the hospital because I got the letter, hello! But how dumb was I? Here I sat at the Breast Cancer clinic, being asked to for a mammogram, and it still had not registered that there may be a problem—the penny had not dropped.

So there I returned to Ayulie and Demi, and together we plodded along to go for the mammogram.

Ayulie and Demi had to wait outside while I went in for the mammogram. They were such good kids, terribly well behaved. They just sat outside reading magazines, keeping themselves busy. Bless!

After the mammogram I was told that I had to go for an ultrasound. I was not happy at all. It seemed too much of a bother when I could be doing something more important with my day. But I reluctantly went for the ultrasound.

Again, I cannot begin to tell you how naïve I was. As I lay down for the ultrasound, the consultant chatted with me and started talking about cancer. I was not in the least bit bothered. Yet again, the penny had not dropped. At the time I had no idea I was actually looking at the cancer tumour.

The lump was self-evident. I saw the calcifications on the left side of my breast, but had no idea what they were or meant.

I guess I could say ignorance is bliss. Not knowing enabled me to carry on with the examination without any fear or worry whatsoever.

The consultant doing the ultrasound then told me that the examination would take a bit longer than I thought, and that I had to go for another mammogram and come back to him. He would speak with the kids to tell them I would be a bit longer. The kids took it in stride again, without winging or complaining, amazingly well behaved.

On my part, I was just hmm, a bit, hmmm. There are no words to describe it. I did not want to be there, that sums it up nicely. Why would I?

I was asking myself, at what point does something that was meant to be a cyst take such a long time to examine?

My examination took not twenty minutes, but two hours twenty minutes. You would have thought I would suspect there might just be a problem. But no, I did not suspect a thing. I still had Ayulie and Demi with me, and I was more concerned that we should be spending the day doing something more interesting than being in the hospital. After the examination I was asked to see my consultant again. By the time I had got to his office downstairs he had already received the ultrasound report.

Once I sat down, he asked me, 'Who did you come with today?'

I replied, 'I came with my son and my niece.'

Then he asked, 'Do you drive?'

'Yes,' I replied.

He continued, 'When you come for the results of your mammogram and ultrasound, do not drive, and come with an adult.'

Finding that terribly amusing, I said, 'When I come back I will drive and may try to come back with an adult.'

The last thing I remember saying was asking him why he said this—it was not as if I were going to die or something. He smiled and I left his office.

From that day onwards my life changed. From one fleeting moment, my son's dream led to me doing a self-breast examination, which led to me taking the time to go to my GP, who referred me to the breast cancer unit. I was not to know that there was a new journey, a new challenge and a new chapter in my life about to unfold.

If my GP did not have a three-hour Saturday surgery I would never have gone to see him. As a single parent, the small mystery of a lump in my breast was the least of my worries. At no moment had I felt really unwell. I was doing a good job at work, my boss was happy with my performance and I was managing a great team. My legal practice course was going very well. I had just completed the first academic year. One year nearer to my dream, I had absolutely nothing to complain about. And Ayulie was truly amazing. At that point in my life I believed I was in Heaven on earth, in paradise. I was content and even very happy, proud to be a single mum doing the simple things while trying to improve myself, and enjoying the journey to my final destination.

It never occurred to me that maybe that was just my plan, and maybe there was just another plan, or perhaps I should say another route, for me to take. My plan was not the plan the Creator had for me, and in an instant, just as all the pieces of my jigsaw finally started to fit, from nowhere the rug was pulled from under my feet. The jigsaw scattered.

Talk about going on a roller coaster ride! Less than ten days after seeing the breast cancer consultant, I was sent an appointment letter to see him for the result. I called my sister and asked if she was free on the day I had to go to the hospital. I did not elaborate on the details of the appointment. How could I? I didn't even know what was going on. Luckily for me, Thelma happened to have that day off work to look after Demi, her daughter, and Ayulie. So she agreed to come with me. I let her know that I had been asked not to drive that day, and so she would be the one who had to drive to and from the hospital even though she was technically my escort. Nice, eh!

My sister is also a parent and a chartered psychologist. As siblings, we have had our ups and downs and do not always agree. But no matter the argument, no matter the disagreement, my son and her daughter always come first, and we never disagreed about the welfare and wellbeing of our children.

I guess during this period my subconscious began to tell me that something may be wrong, but I was not excessively concerned. However, the night before I had to go to the hospital I did not sleep very well. I was uneasy for some strange reason. The uncertainty is worse than the actual knowing. At least once you know what you have got to contend with, you can begin the process of contending.

On the day of the appointment, my sister, her daughter, and my son and I went to the hospital to see the consultant. The kids could not go into the consultant's room, but Thelma and I both sat down inside. Then the consultant said, 'I am sure by now you know you have got breast cancer?'

Well, actually, I did not know.

Thelma looked at me, touched my knee and burst out crying. I just listened to what more he had to say.

'You have stage III breast cancer in your right breast, but there are calcifications in your left breast. They think it is cancer but would like to get a second opinion.' He wanted to refer me to another hospital to have a biopsy.

After that we were passed on to the breast care nurse, who took us to a room to ask if we need counselling. This is so: Thelma is a Chartered Psychologist and counsels clients on a regular basis. When I was being given all the oomph–leaflets on breast cancer and such—I said, 'Maybe my sister could do with counselling,' because she was crying so hard. If you had seen her you would have thought she was the one who had just been told she had breast cancer. Only now did I realize the impact that cancer has on families. We declined counselling, as I really did not need it at the time.

The kids were waiting for us. How on earth do you break the news to kids who have come with you to the hospital, kids who have always been with you through thick and thin, sick and sin? We as a family had not experienced anything like this before, and God knows we did not have the skills to handle it, but thank God we were all naïve and totally ignorant of what was ahead of us.

When we came out of the patients' room (this is the room they take patients and family to give them all the leaflets and let those who need a good cry, cry in private), Thelma had calmed down. The kids had questions, in particular Ayulie. 'Mum, so what did they say is wrong with you?'

First, we told the kids that I had to go for a blood test and X-ray. As I told Thelma, since we were already at the hospital I might as well get the tests done. I just couldn't be asked to come back to do them another day; it would be too much trouble. However, Ayulie and Demi were persistent, continuing to ask what the consultant had told me. At that point, I had no choice. In between having a blood test and X-ray, we told our children that I had been diagnosed with cancer. Ayulie was visibly upset, while Demi handled it well. Thelma was still in shock.

I had informed my boss that I was going to get the results of my test. He told me to let him know the minute I heard them, so before I left the hospital I called him on my mobile phone. He said he was sorry to hear about my diagnosis, as he was hoping it would be one of the nine out of ten cases where the lump turns out to be benign.

I will never forget the journey home because it was so funny. At the end of the day, no matter what challenges life has to offer you have to find a place to laugh. In our family, when the going gets tough, we laugh. Humour relieves us and makes the challenge ahead slightly more bearable.

As Thelma was driving, I told her I thought I was the one who was supposed to be crying. I thought the purpose of her coming was so she could take in all the information while I just cried. But no, she cries and I have to take in all the information! We both burst out laughing. It was very ironic, and at that moment I was not going to take myself or the situation seriously.

Thelma goes, 'So why did you not tell me that you had breast cancer? You know I don't know how to handle these things, I don't like being shocked.'

Her reply made me laugh even more. It was not like I had any idea before the doctor told me! The fact remains, this laughter helped us prepare, and we really did need to be in a good place mentally, physically and emotionally for the road ahead. We were just two black mothers trying our hardest to do the best for our children and ourselves. We knew then we had no choice but to hack it. The laughter was good.

The truth of the matter was I did not actually feel anything.

***

These past journal 'entries' have been written completely from the benefit of the perspective that time gives, from my memories. Now I will share the journaling I did at the time, without knowing what the future would hold—my experience, unfolding a day at a time:

10 August

Oh, please. No one should have to go through all that poking, probing, etc. Finally D-day has arrived. I went for my assessment with Ayulie and Demi at the hospital.

August 19

I did not sleep very well on 18 August. The not knowing, the uncertainty, is actually worse than knowing. As I said before, at least when you know what you have to contend with, you can actually begin to sort out the problem.

Today I had to go to King's College hospital for the biopsy and second opinion.

That was not a pleasant experience. I had to lie face down on a bed. The bed had a hole in it, through which I had to put my left breast. There a biopsy was taken. It hurt like crazy, and I could see the calcifications in all their glory staring back at me.

Looking back, I am so glad I did not have any knowledge of what the scan meant. I think if I had known then what I know now, the outcome would have been so different. I would have allowed nature to take its course. I do not think I would have bothered with treatment.

Wow, it has been a roller coaster of emotions since I got the result of the biopsy. For the right breast, it is a pretty straightforward surgery to remove the lump and lymph nodes. My left breast is pre-cancerous.

I telephoned the office to inform my line manager and team. They were all extremely supportive. On my way back, I decided to stop over at Thelma's from Kings College Hospital, as I was in no mood to go straight home. I did feel a bit tired and weary. The diagnosis just seemed so much of an inconvenience.

I only prayed that this whole situation did not shatter my dreams of becoming a solicitor. I would not allow it to do that. I was not mentally prepared to change my strategy or to think of something else to do with my life. I had put so much effort into obtaining my law degrees that I honestly thought I would do something silly if this inconvenience did not allow me to finish.

I finally told the rest of my family and friends that I had been diagnosed with breast cancer. All this while it had only been me, Thelma, Demi and Ayulie who were aware, as it was just the four of us going to the hospital for my tests and X-rays.

The family has all been terribly supportive and particularly prayerful. At times like this one has to call on our Creator, because really, one has to look for strength and courage outside one's self, especially when words are not enough. It has been comforting to know that I was not alone. Yet in addition, it is scary to see their reactions and know that life for them would still go on no matter what.

I just wish I could understand how I am feeling, because I don't know how and what I feel about the situation. It seems as though this is happening to someone else. The best way to describe it is that it is as though I have been given a role in a play and am acting a part.

I cannot identify with what is happening to me. The question, or maybe the answer, is that I seem to be in a state of denial. I am not in the least bit concerned or anxious as to the outcome of this cancer. Maybe it is because I believe life is overrated. I will depart from this earth one day and if it has to be now, so be it.

But on the other side of the scales, I have a taken on the responsibility of having a child. As a consequence, it is my continuing responsibility to ensure that I remain on this earth long enough to see him through to an age where he can fend for himself.

At least my friends and family have been amazing, and this is pre-operation. Only God knows what will happen post-operation.

My friend Sara, who studies with me at college, sent me a beautiful bouquet of flowers today. It put a huge smile on my face even as it reduced me to tears. How touching. Life has been good. Like everyone else, I have bad times with the good ones, but that is life.

Right now I wish I could feel something. I wish I could cry some more, I wish some form of emotion would appear. But nothing is happening. I wonder how many others feel this way? Breast cancer is no longer an ailment that kills. It is curable, as if I have a common cold. Nor are my symptoms particularly bad. I am full of energy, my mind is clear. I just lack any form of emotion.

I guess it is the philosopher in me saying that if this does not kill me, something else will. Whatever happens, one day you will meet your Creator.

I have done plenty of talking, telling my friends. They think I am strong. Let the truth be known: I am not fussed one bit. I am also not upset. Perhaps a bit restless, though. Right now, all I want to do is go on a holiday alone or with one of my friends.

My mind wanders and I am back to the cancer situation. I was given much literature to read, including information about reconstructive surgery.

Now, let me tell you my thoughts on reconstructive surgery. I am definitely going to have breast reconstruction because I am so vain. I cannot help but smile when I say I am vain, but it is true. Furthermore, after all is said and done, I am the one who will have to live with my body, no one else. I am not going to have a scar to constantly remind me of my ailment when I live in a country, the UK, where I can have reconstruction. Hello, I have paid my taxes and dues. I am not mad. A decent 'boob job' will do me just fine. And the good thing is I can have immediate reconstruction. Yippee!!!

20 August

Last night I slept soundly for the first time since 28 July. Think I needed that much deserved sleep. It is well. Before I went to bed I finally read all the information on breast cancer and the options available for breast reconstruction. It is times like this that you thank your lucky stars that you can read. Better yet, the literature is in plain English, easy to read and easy to understand. It has made it so much clearer for me.

Being one who thinks best during the middle of the night, I was finally able to understand why I am not feeling any emotion. It is because I am not scared. I always tell my friends, 'Do not let fear be your guide. But let God be your guide.' In this case, God is my guide, definitely not fear. If that were not the case, I would not have found the lump at stage 3, risk factor critical. There is no reason for fear now.

I have read the breast reconstruction options and it is most likely I will go for the thigh, hip or buttocks option. Maybe a year down the line I will do the second breast reconstruction. Let's see how we get on. I am still not pleased to go for the radiotherapy and chemotherapy treatment. They sound ghastly and also a bit tedious.

Something else cropped up from the literature I read and that is the symptoms of cancer. I did not show any of the classic symptoms. The only symptom I showed—extreme fatigue—was not stressed or highlighted. After all, I already had plenty of reasons to feel exhausted. Everything relied on that chance self-examination I made at the end of July.

The good thing is my brother Dukuye who is experienced in alternative therapy, has offered to do a healing for me before and after radiotherapy and chemotherapy if I decide to go down that route.

I think I understand why I am not scared of the operation, either. I have so much help and support around that I am actually blessed. Along with being blessed, I have my faith. My spirit is getting stronger and I feel capable of handling the tasks ahead of me.

I have to focus on passing my exams and doing my PLR2, or Practical Legal Research. I am more than determined to get the exams out of the way. Not only do I no longer feel tired anymore, my energy has even returned.

It is amazing when something like this happens and you suddenly begin to understand who you are.

In my case, I have always known that my appearance is important to me. This time is no exception. I am concerned about losing my hair—that is not going to happen! End of discussion! I will not even think on it! And I am concerned about my breasts and will do everything possible to keep them just the way they are. It is bad enough I have already had a major surgery some years ago, how am I supposed to now have a mastectomy? I might as well have all my insides removed. Gosh!

This is another interesting challenge I have to tackle all by myself, without a partner. How many more things will I have to do on my own? Who knows? There is one good thing about going it alone, and that is that I do not have to think of what my supposed 'partner' or boyfriend or spouse thinks. I do not have to have any operation based on what someone else wants or would like. My body is my concern, and I will make the choices about it.

I am able to identify with the photographs of breast reconstruction patients this time round. The first time I had a look at the pictures my tummy churned and I thought I was going to be violently sick. I had to put all the literature away, only to bring it out now, three weeks later.

It is three in the morning and I am reading and reviewing the pictures and literature all over. I can relate to these photographs of breasts. They seem so realistic. They do not show all the nice, uplifted breasts that are plastered in magazines and on the television. They showed breasts that have sagged slightly through breastfeeding or age. Honestly, these breasts are true to African women. Thank goodness for that! The lack of nipples is a bit worrying, though.

I know I will come out unscathed because I will not be dwelling on all the negative things that could possibly happen. Not only that, but I have absolutely no intention of leaving my legal practice course unfinished. My self-indulgence and self-pity in this matter is OVER! I will finish my coursework and I will not be retaking any more exams. This disease should not be happening, but being lazy and sorry for myself because of it simply is not an option.

21 August

Another wonderful night. Nothing compares to having a good night's rest. This morning I woke up thinking I could take on the world. I got up early to go do my banking, paying bills and more bills. It seems as though that is all we ever do in England. Well, I decided to do my banking in Croydon Whitgift Shopping Centre.

Just as I parked my car, my mobile phone bill went off. It was Mel, from an agency I was with, telling me I had got a job.

Quick flash back: I went for a job interview on August 15, two days before my cancer diagnosis.

Mel told me my interview was successful and I had got the job. Wow! The job was three miles from home and would pay much more than I am currently earning. I could not believe my ears. I was over the moon and reduced to tears. Not all happy tears, either. Because of my cancer diagnosis, I was hoping I would not be chosen for the job. I knew the position, a Senior Property Manager in charge of a leasehold portfolio, would be challenging, although it was also something that was up my street. I accepted the offer despite my cancer diagnosis, because I know my cancer is only a temporary inconvenience. My current boss has even said he knew I would get the job, as he has so much faith in my abilities. I knew I did a good interview, although you never know if the person interviewing you wants you or likes you until you hear back. There are so many hurdles to jump before you are actually offered a job.

Upon receiving this job offer, I simply began to walk on water. The fact remains, I have not been upset about the cancer situation. I have done my research, and through it I have formed some idea what treatment I am willing to go through and treatment I will not be touching. All of a sudden, life seems good. Being offered the job has been simply a validation that I know what I am doing. A £10,000 salary increase is nothing to be sniffed at, with or without cancer!

What a blessing the good Lord has bestowed upon me.

24 August

I have not written anything in my journal for a couple of days now. Nothing much is happening. Today I went to college to do some revision. College is becoming a struggle, mentally and emotionally. The only good thing today was my stumbling across the relevant case I need for my PLR2. That indeed was a miracle. All things being equal, I ought to be able to hand in my assessment on the due date.

I am still utterly, utterly confused about how the new job offer is going to pan out. I want it badly. It ticks all the right boxes: proximity, dealing 100% with leasehold properties I know I will do well in. Yet I wonder if my expectations are unrealistic. Can I take a new job while weathering my exams and this cancer diagnosis?

The truth is, I remind myself, if you don't take risks you will never grow or never know. I only pray that whatever is happening, with my health, my studies, and my career, my guardian angel will look after me and protect me. God knows, I am only trying to improve my fortune. I will continue to take my chances in life. If I had not, or should I say if I had never attempted to improve my lot, I would not be where I am today.

Please Lord, do not abandon me at this time.

I hope something good comes out of my diagnosis. I will have to try to do something creative, turn this situation into something positive.

26 August

Today I'm feeling a bit down. Just got another call to confirm my appointment at Kings for my final biopsy. I am not living in hope. This seems like just another test to be endured.

I think I started feeling low after the phone call. It brings it home that this breast cancer thingy is actually real and is happening to me, and that sooner rather than later I will lose some body parts. I cannot say I am looking forward to it—surgery is not the most exciting prospect.

One thing I have finally decided is that I will not keep on laughing and smiling if I don't want to. Forget that! I will try to maintain a positive attitude, as that's the best thing I can do for myself. At the same time, I will not put up with anyone telling me what I am not interested in hearing. At the end of the day, it is my journey, my story, and I have to live it. I must take the journey on my own. Nobody will want to trade places with me at this moment, so I am not going to listen to any of their unsolicited advice. That includes putting on a show of happiness if I am not really feeling it.

Another thing that is making me low is how I've been thinking, and these thoughts have brought me back to earth with a big crash. I now know that I cannot accept the job offer as a Senior Property Manager. I need my sick leave, I need to heal, and I don't think I will be able to deal with the added pressure of worrying about a new job.

Oh, but it hurts, my tears are flowing. I need the job, I know how to do the job, I want the job, I need the extra income. Why did this have to happen now, and to me? Oh why, Lord, why me? I lament; see my tears, my Lord and my God, hear my cry, feel my pain, my sorrow, my grief. I beg you Lord, release me.

It is a painful decision for me to make, because I could seriously do with the extra money. It would help me and Ayulie so much, but alas! What on earth can I do? Health is also wealth. If I am healthy, I can become wealthy in time. If I am wealthy but have no health, I will not be able to enjoy the wealth anyway. It is the Lord who giveth and the Lord who taketh away. So the Lord will replace what is being taken away from me when I return to good health. Yes, when I am healthy again. The problem is that so much uncertainty surrounds this ailment, and I just cannot plan too far ahead. I do not know when I will be booked for surgery, I do not know how I will react to treatment. These are the biggest uncertainties, and these are exactly the things that need to be planned for. It's so frustrating, and makes it hard to feel hopeful.

If I had my way now, I would not even bother having surgery. I would let the ailment take its toll and simply enjoy the rest of my life.

Unfortunately or fortunately, I do not have a choice. I have to get better for the sake of my son.

Faith and Fatalism

It is very difficult to explain the spiritual emotional and physical pain that you go through when you are confronted with an illness you have absolutely no knowledge of. I had no tools to work with. I did not know what to expect.

At the time of my diagnosis, my only knowledge and understanding of cancer was that it was an ugly and painful illness. That it would gradually eat away at you. That you would suffer a painful death no matter what you did or did not do. It would come for you like a thief in the night, slowly robbing you of all your senses one at a time.

The few people I knew who had been diagnosed with cancer had all passed away. A friend's mother, my first cousin, and a few others, the acquaintances you hear about in passing. All I ever heard was 'Oh! So-and-so, such-and-such a person has died, passing away after a long battle with cancer.'

More importantly, I heard that cancer, once you had it, could return and grow. Now I know the word is metastasis. It means the spread of cancer to other parts of the body. A word I cannot pronounce up till now!

It is astonishing, indeed astounding, to realise how much and just what kind of information we store in our subconscious minds. I believe my subconscious mind decided to process the little information I had about cancer to guide my thoughts. I also strongly believe that during this time, I became extremely intuitive without knowing it. To this day, my intuition is heightened.

I have mentioned earlier that I alone had to look after my son Ayulie as he grew up. He struggled with childhood aliments. He was a baby, he was young, but it was so painful to witness so much hurt experienced by any human being, let alone a young child and my own son. I nursed him to good health, but it took a toll on my own health now and again. That was the least of my worries when my son was unwell. I did not feel pain even when I was unwell while looking after him. I had to be strong for him. It was non-negotiable. I prayed so hard to the bearer and carrier of his pain and cross. I will never forget the day I spoke to the Lord in the quietness of our home, begging God to release my child from the pain and anguish of his conditions. In that moment, the physical manifestation of the Lord came to me. I felt someone or something physically remove the burden from my shoulders, and I believe from that day onwards, I became stronger and my son began to get better. Yet it had been a slow and trying illness. It began when he was two years of age, and he did not get better till he was seven years old.

When I say in my journal that I would not have even bothered with surgery, that I would let the cancer take its course and just enjoy my life to a certain extent, one might say, Why not fight it, Alero? Why not do all that you can do to ensure you live a bit longer?

True, there is no denying that this would be a very good and reasonable way to look at it. But our past life and present define our actions and reactions. Our histories and our hearts are not always perfectly reasonable. The choices they help us make certainly do not always make sense to other people, even when they are clear to ourselves—the only people most directly affected.

My thoughts were all over the place, but one thing I wondered was if cancer was really the grim reaper just coming to take me away. It was not even the most frightening though. After all, was I not twice blessed that I knew what was going to take me away? Was I not twice blessed that I had been given notice that my Maker was waiting for me to return to the place where I had come? Wouldn't it be fair to say God was telling me that I now needed to enjoy my time on earth?

On the other hand, I could have interpreted my diagnosis as God telling me the illness I had been diagnosed with was not life threatening. My son's dream had prompted me to make a self-examination that caught the cancer in my breasts in time for treatment. With treatment, I could get through it. I was merely up for a challenge.

To this day, I believe my ailment was an awakening to live life to the full. To take one day at a time.

My choice, though, to fight or to let cancer take its course, was made easy by my son. I could not bear to leave him alone at an age where he still needed to have a mother in his life. It was a no brainer.

But I would like to say, I also recognised it was my life, my choice. Either choice I could have made would have been a good choice, a positive choice, and not a defeatist choice. I am a firm believer in the quality of life and not the quantity of life.

***

27 August
It is 8:15 a.m. and I am just about to leave home to sit an assessment. I hope I pass it. I have put in the best effort I possibly can in revision. All I have to do now is stay calm. If I am able to avoid panic, I am sure I will able to scrape through. The mark is going to be capped anyway, so there is really no pressure to get an excellent grade, just one good enough to pass.

I feel better today, albeit still not terribly pleased about the thought of having part of my body amputated. What is the point of having my 'boobs' mutilated? I think it is wrong on so many levels! I have to think seriously whether I honestly want to undergo the treatment.

In my case, after my previous major surgeries, I feel like I might as well have a sex change and become a man. I cannot think of anything so unfeminine. If all the things that make you a woman are no longer there, then I would like someone explain to me the purpose of undergoing treatment to save what is left. Physically you may feel better, yet what about emotionally and mentally? It is dreadful.

It does not help that I am not in a relationship of any sort. In a way it is okay, as I really do not know how many people are prepared to stick by you when critical illness or major tragedies happen. Not everyone could solve such problems or even face them. In addition, as I am on my own I don't have to think of some other person pointing out that all my essential body parts are not there. Or is all this fuss over it a figment of my vivid imagination?

Yet I believe being single is not a blessing when you get to a certain age. It certainly does not help when you fall ill, no matter how minor the ailment.

Being single does not mean you cannot handle difficult situations—the stress of managing for yourself may simply shorten your life span, maybe not, who knows? Worrying about it certainly won't help! However, the fact is that you have to muster up so much energy to achieve anything on your own; you have to be self-motivated. It can sometimes be a tall order to be a singleton. If you have a religion or a faith, or tons of friends, or just love yourself so much, then you may be able to stay stronger for longer. But being single when you'd rather not can be tough.

Being on my own with the ailment is a new terrain. I do have some sources of strength, though. Throughout it all, God will be my comforter and my protector. He will never fail me.

I don't hate the ailment. It is happening to so many women all over the world. I am only another statistic. Yet I just can't come to terms with the agony one has to go through.

I am so irritated that I will have to be home recovering for goodness knows how many weeks. God give me the strength. One thing I do know is I am going to be so bored, at home by myself day in and day out, aside from when I have to go for radio or chemo. Now that is what's going to kill me—the boredom. It will start to get dark early, and winter darkness can make things seem worse than they really are. But I am not even going to pretend to be happy or sad, positive or negative. I will simply go with the flow as my mood takes me. I will not even try to be brave.

Anyway, I must be out of here to sit the exam. God grant me a clear mind and retentive memory to get through this paper. Let's see if I can dispose of this exam pretty damn quick!

28 August

Got the exam out of the way. Thank goodness I sat it! All in all, it was not a bad paper.

I've been busy all week, but at least I have been distracted from my ailment. Oftentimes, I still do not think it is really happening to me. I genuinely do not know the magnitude of what is going on in my body. I just know that my weight is dropping off really fast.

31 August

Another biopsy at the Princess Royal. For crying out loud, this is so inconvenient. Yes, I know everything is being done to make sure they get it right; yes, I know it is for my own sake. Tell me all about it. I still wish I could ask everyone to go away and stop bothering about treatment. Gosh, what a palaver!

3 September

Over the past two weeks, things have returned to some form of normality. During the summer holidays, I have spent quality time with Ayulie. We've gone sight-seeing in London in between my trips to the hospital.

My appetite is gone now, and I am losing weight rapidly. And meanwhile I am always touching my lump, as if I hope and expect that one day I will find it has vanished into thin air. Good things have happened. Yes. My son Jnr has come to live with us. Well, Jnr is not my biological son. He is my distant relation. So as an African, I call him my son and he calls me Mum. That's all there is to it. Works well for us!

I am really so pleased to have Jnr. He has come as a ray of sunshine. Jnr is 15 years old and the most delightful, respectful, thoughtful loving child any mother could wish for. He is talented too, simply brilliant. His real mum has been truly blessed to have him as a son. I am blessed that she has been generous enough to allow me be his second mum.

Ayulie is blessed to have a brother, too. God works in mysterious ways. He gives you and sends to you what you need in His time. God knows we need Jnr in our household. Till the end of time, Jnr, you will be loved by me, your second mum for all eternity.

Jnr has brought joy to our home.

And I have needed this joy, too, because not all has been well with me.

Today, after weeks of soul searching, I finally told the agency I would not be able to take up the Senior Property Manager position. The agency had called me five times wanting to know when I would start. I had told Mel at the agency about my diagnosis.

I did a silly thing that made me feel good, though. On August 20 I got the contract of employment, signed it and sent it back to the Human Resources department. I just need to see the salary I was going to be paid, the money that I was worth. I had to see it in writing. And let me say, when I did see I was proud of myself for getting into that pay bracket! It was a huge feat.

But I cried that night for the very first time, real sobbing, heart-wrenching tears. I did not cry because of the ailment. I cried because I felt weary and tired and could not see the light at the end of the tunnel. Reality—my world collapsing around me—was too hard to bear.

The next day was worse, because the agency called me to inform me that the employers would consider my ailment if I could give a definite start. Mel had got back to them and told them about my situation. They were more than delighted to wait for me to receive treatment and start work with them afterwards. On that basis, I told Mel that sounded good. I agreed with it in principle, but I could not know how long a time my recovery process might entail. I broke down yet again as I told the agency I could not give a start date. I was not in any position to do that. There were too many unknowns. I had to let the job go.

On Saturday, I went for a healing session with Dukuye. That was an interesting experience. Good thing I went with an open mind!

My brother has received training in Western Reiki, which seeks to treat the whole body instead of specific areas. The atmosphere in the room where his consultation took place was calm, and protected from both outside noise and bright light. Wearing loose, comfortable clothing, I lay down on a massage table and relaxed.

Reiki is deeply relaxing therapy. It is also a spiritual practice, developed in 1922 by Japanese Buddhist Mikao Usui, which has since been adapted by various teachers of varying traditions. It uses a technique commonly called 'palm healing' or 'hands-on healing'. The belief is that energy will flow through the practitioner's hands as they are placed on or held near a potential recipient's body. Some teachings say the practitioner's intention is important to the process, while others claim Reiki energy is intelligent, and will be drawn to the site of whatever injury or illness needs healing. Like most alternative medicine, there is no scientific evidence to suggest whether it is helpful for treating any condition one way or the other. Yet Dukuye had offered, and I think today's treatment has helped me find some peace and understanding. At the least it was something different to try!

Lying there for approximately an hour, in silence, and having healing hands on my face, head and feet was a new one for me. Dukuye's hands would rest over a part of my body for a few minutes before moving on to the next position. The experience on my face was rather fascinating. With Dukuye's palms over my eyes, I felt I could see many images, especially of colours.

The first colour that appeared was white. It revealed all the cancer cells. When Dukuye's hands moved down to my chin, sunset colours appeared: magenta, red and orange. After that, the colour blue appeared. Here the scene was a road or path strewn with many pebbles, and at the end of it was the sky, light blue and dark blue. Other scenes flashed through my mind: a beach and a little child waving goodbye to me.

I had my conversation with God. He knows how I feel and what I want, but as the adage goes, what man proposes, God disposes. I know now that God knows how strongly I feel about not taking radiotherapy and chemotherapy.

At the end of the healing session, Dukuye brought out a deck of cards, called the Tarot of Marseilles. The 78 cards of the Tarot are split into two groups, 22 trumps of major arcana and 56 suits of minor arcana. The major arcana are very metaphorical, depicting colourful characters like the fool, the empress, the lovers, the wheel of fortune, the tower (or the house of God), and death (or 'the trump without a name'). A specific symbolic meaning is attached to each card.

I slowly shuffled the cards and cut the deck before giving back to Dukuye. Dukuye then laid out the cards facedown, making a spread, from which I chose my card. He placed the selected card from left to right and began his interpretation.

The card I had picked was The Hanged Man, or Death Temptation. On the card was a picture of someone ready to hang him- or herself. Dukuye's interpretation of the card was that it means being weary, 'fed up.' And the card actually put my thoughts and feelings into words! The meaning of the card was exactly how I felt at the moment. My state of mind was one big 'Urgh,' and I was terribly fed up. Nor I did not feel sorry for myself pointlessly. In fact, I have every right to feel fed up and to dislike what is going on in my life. I did not ask for the ailment.

Anyway, the card also stated that death means a rebirth as long as you are willing to let go. To embrace change and do things differently. Not something I had considered so much. My state of mind was blocking creativity.

The Divinatory meaning of the Hanged Man: The Hanged Man is a card that relates to self-sacrifice in order to attain a higher spiritual goal. The upside-down position can reflect that this person is an outcast of society and tends to follow his or her own inner voice. The fact that the man is suspended upside down can represent a time of transition, limbo or a pause in life, until something or someone is sacrificed for the greater gain of others. A negative slant on the card would represent poor health or weakness of will. It suggests patience, and warns to watch out for paths that lead in a bad direction.

I would like to reiterate I went along with all this because Dukuye is my brother. He is also a meditation practitioner and a massage therapist. Plus this was free for me, so why not?—I laugh. I trusted him, and that is all that mattered. I was not expecting answers and I did not go with questions. I went with an open mind. It was not going to add to or take away my cancer. But as the adage goes, 'nothing ventured, nothing gained.' I am not suggesting or recommending Reiki to anyone. I just know at this moment in time, I have found some peace and understanding.

Afterwards, Dukuye asked me how I felt and what I had seen. As a practitioner, I believe it crossed his mind that I could have told him what a load of 'b*******' it had been, but the fact that I had experienced a reaction meant to him that he had done a good job. Even if alternative medicine is not scientifically proven, I feel it has a place in healing for many people, including me.

So that has been the past few days.

Today is Sunday, 3 September, and I do not feel any better. I just want to be left alone to wallow in self-pity and indulge in my own misery. Let the truth be known: I genuinely do not like feeling this way. I'm not choosing to feel this way. It's just happening. Maybe it is a way of reaching out to cancer. Who knows? But whatever the reason behind my situation, I am so not happy.

Like I did before, I want to go away—to take a holiday and have space and time to perhaps gather my thoughts and prepare for my operation. I am not fully prepared to have my body tampered with. I am not prepared to go through this ridiculous pain. I am not prepared for anything in the world at the moment.

I cannot see the beauty around me, because everything seems so bleak. I cannot see my own future. I am tired, very tired. I feel like I have lost everything and do not have the energy to start anything again. Where on earth am I going to get my strength? There is only so much a person can take; there are only so many blows one's body and mind can take. The good thing is, I know with all certainty I will not lose my mind and go insane. Nope! That is so not going to happen. I am smiling, telling myself that will be very foolish. Besides, I don't feel that weak and vulnerable right now. Tired, yes, but sane.

Thank goodness for this journal. I know by the time I get to the last page, happier memories will have been written down. Rome was not built in a day and I know my cancer recovery journey may take years.

5 September

It has been said, and it is so true, that every day is different. When the morning comes, yesterday becomes the past, and the morning is the present. And sometimes the present is a gift!

Today I finally returned to work after being away for two weeks. My colleagues were really nice to me and terribly understanding. What a difference support and encouragement can make. Even though I did not sleep well the night before, I seemed to have plenty of energy. I have not been able to eat well, either. My weight is already dropping off, not because I am intentionally on a diet— except for that fad called the 'anxiety diet.'

At work, I am able to speak to colleagues about the cancer diagnosis. I actually feel different. Being away from work has given me time to process the fact that I truly have cancer. I know I won't be able to stay at work much longer— I'll need time off for my treatments, but how much, I do not know. All the same, I am also processing the fact that if things were different, I might not have returned to my current place of employment after all. If not for this cancer, I would not have had to turn down the offer of another job.

I believe I have found a new appreciation towards my employer and colleagues. When you are in a position that makes you ponder your mortality, I guess you begin to appreciate the good, the bad, and the ugly all at the same time. The bad and the ugly matter less, especially when everyone seems so very nice. But the kindness of others also made me realize the gravity of the illness I had been diagnosed with.

I remember going to a mandatory in-house training session on Equality and Diversity soon after my diagnosis. Over the course of the day, I said to the trainer, who I knew in passing from previous training sessions, and as we got to talking I mentioned that I had cancer. He told me, 'Alero, cancer is one of the four critical illnesses that your employers are not allowed to discriminate against. It is not a means-tested ailment.' The bottom line, he made it very clear to me, is that I am protected by law. It was very reassuring to be equipped with that knowledge early on. Sometimes a few choice words delivered at the right time can be so meaningful.

The only problem is I am now beginning to feel very tearful. I guess it is good in a way, because it is a kind of release and acceptance.

A colleague of mine, Rosemary, also has breast cancer. She sent me an email telling me she is having the feeling of phantom breast—how sad.

Today I have also returned to college for year 2 of my part-time Legal Practice Course. For this I've got mixed emotions. Yet more than ever before, I know that I am not going to quit. Instead, I will try my utmost to get through the course.

In a way I feel stronger and I think being able to prepare for the cancer treatment is helping. I am trying not to think too much about it, but I am conscious that cancer is inside of me. Naughty, naughty cells.

I feel lighter and happier from the support I am getting from colleagues at work and college.

10 September

I have not written much this week. Things are back to normal. My sons are at school, just like me. Again we are busy, busy, busy. Life goes on.

I got an infection on my left breast from one of the biopsies, so I had to go to my GP for some antibiotics. He also prescribed sleeping pills.

Sleep is becoming extremely elusive. How can I sleep?

13 September

Time is going by so quickly. Like the tide, it waits for no man.

It was back to the hospital today. I went with my sister to discuss and finalise my treatment with my consultant, Mr Singh at Princess Royal Orpington.

We finally agreed I will have a double mastectomy with immediate bilateral reconstruction. I was a bit worried that I will not be able to have it done. It has been a long and winding route to this decision.

The morning is different from the evening, the evening is different from the night, and the night is different from the next day.

In the beginning I was against any form of treatment, including a mastectomy.

I do not know when my thoughts began to change, when I began to realize that I had to do something. I just know that something must have happened to start the shift. Just maybe, I could not lie down and fade away without giving it my best shot. I try my utmost best in everything I do. And this time is no exception. I have to put my best foot forward and just get on with it.

So it was decided: I would receive treatment. Yet I was not too sure as to what treatment I wanted to have.

At the time of my diagnosis I was given so much literature to read, it was a real literary overload! With my head still reeling, my feelings still numb, my body and very soul exhausted, I was not prepared to read the literature at all. However, one night—the 19th August, around one in the morning—I mustered up the will power to read the literature on breast reconstruction. It explained how on a single breast would be reconstructed. At no point did in my reading did I see anything about how I could have a double mastectomy and immediate bilateral reconstruction.

I highlighted the section on reconstruction, though, to discuss with my Mr Singh. As a consequence of this gap in the literature, I went in uncertain whether my choice of treatment would be available to me.

I also told Mr Singh that I did not want to have radiotherapy and chemotherapy. He told me I could get away with not having radiotherapy, but I would have to have chemotherapy, in any event. I guess it is a fair compromise.

Mr Singh told me that I would not have the surgery done at Princess Royal, as the particular surgery I have requested will need to involve plastic surgeons. The plastic surgeons in question are at Guy's and St Thomas' hospital. On that note, I had to wait for an appointment to see them at St Thomas'.

I feel so relieved that I can have the surgery that I am hardly bothered with how it will delay the start of my treatment.

For the first time in this process, I feel I have started regaining control over what I now call my cancer.

From the time I was diagnosed, I let my cancer take hold of me. I let it control my thoughts. Today was a dawn; today I took control of my cancer and its treatment.

Along with the opportunity for taking control, I feel thankful to have so much support from friends and family. Thelma, has been extremely helpful, as have my sons Ayulie and Jnr. My lovely niece Demi, my friends Teju, Gbadero, Bimbo, Kunbo, Amaka, Gaby, Tony, Lucky, Josef, Toritseju, my cousin Buge, my supportive and helpful co-worker Rosemary, Jumai, Chudi, and Thandi, to name a few. My Auntie Roli and Uncle Godfrey, my mother. I cannot express my gratitude and how touched I am by their thoughts, words and deeds.

14 September
The Bible says it rained for forty days and forty nights. After that it stopped raining. In other words, things must end, nothing can go forever.

Today is another brand new day.

I woke up with a horrible headache, but it is okay. My spirits are high. I have mourned the upcoming loss of my 'boobs,' as I know them, and must now mentally come to terms with the fact that I will have them replaced. I am not in a hurry for the surgery to have them replaced, although I am not sad to lose them, either.

Modern technology is a wonderful thing when it comes to medical treatments, but I am a true victim of modern society and most of its values and ways. This includes our obsession with appearance. I want to look good in order for me to feel good. I am going to make good use of the reconstructive surgery to enhance my appearance. It is a good thing I have never been adverse to plastic surgery!

The good Lord is smiling upon me. My feelings are normal, thank the Lord for that. My faith is strong, but my spirit is even stronger.

I know that I am extremely comfortable, unconditionally comfortable with either way this disease goes. I have finally come to terms with outcomes—and there are only two: either I survive this cancer, or I do not. And I am not in control of either of those outcomes.

The experiences of my life have taught me that sometimes, just sometimes, you have to let go. Once you let go, it is easier to see things clearly.

I saw this happen during my son's struggle with ill health when he was very young and suffering from his allergies and asthma. Now it was my turn. Drawing from my time helping Ayulie, I knew that trying to control what was happening did not really matter. What mattered most was being at peace with myself. And honestly, I did not have to struggle too hard to get to that place of peace.

My cancer is stage 3. With most cancers, stage 4 is considered terminal.

I am not trying to be a hero, to be brave or strong. Instead, I know that what will be, will be.

Finding peace is a gift, but perhaps it should have come earlier. The stress and worry of modern-day living has finally taken its toll. This illness is a wake-up call for me to review the way I have been juggling so many things. I know my body has taken a battering, although honestly, what is new?

What is happening to me, what has happened to me, and what will happen, is certainly nothing new. The path has been walked down before. There have been others before me, and there are those walking along this path with me and there will be others walking down the path after me.

I do not feel sad. It is just another challenge. At least it is going to relieve me of my usual robotic, monotonous routine. Quite a drastic method of relief, but never mind.

It is wonderful how each day brings something different. It would have been pretty awful if we did not have summer, spring, autumn and winter. For every season, there is a reason, and God knows why he has made our lives like this. Along with bringing difference, time is an also a great healer.

Yesterday, knowing I could have the immediate bilateral reconstruction was like a mighty weight being taken off my shoulders. I feel as though I am able to move on with my life. I have to live with my body, after it has all been said and done, so I will do everything that needs to be done to make it a body I am happy living with.

I am moving on to the next stage. Since I have agreed with Mr Singh about having chemotherapy along with my reconstruction, I am now going to concern myself in getting head wraps, beautiful ones, colourful ones, small ones, big ones, so that when I become bald from the treatment I will be able to create my new image. I can't wait. This at least is something for me to look forward to. Worse things happen to people. People die because they do not have the right medical facilities and meanwhile, my God has created me and put me in a good place to be able to face my cancer full on. I say bring it on, and we will see who will triumph. Until God says it is my time, I cannot quit and I cannot and will not give up.

Oh yes, I say to myself, it is your time to reinvent yourself. Now is a good time. I shall use my period of recovery to think creatively and figure out that I want to do with the rest of my natural life. Until then, I will just continue to pray and prepare myself mentally for my surgery and recovery. Through it all I have faith. There is no mountain that is too high to climb. There is no obstacle that cannot be overcome.

I am pleased with the time delay before the surgery, because the wait and preparation are only helping me to form a positive attitude towards this whole cancer saga. Time to think has enabled me to empower myself and gain perspective, realizing that worse things can and could happen.

I love my journal, and writing does help. Putting one's thoughts on paper is a good thing. Thoughts and moods change like the four seasons. You realise when you read what you have written back that some of the thoughts are only suitable for their season. You also learn that thoughts and moods will change when another season comes. It is all for a reason. We cannot stay permanently fixated, we must change. Change helps the mind; it opens it up and allows you to adapt, to deal with other things that come up.

Change is useful. I embrace change all the time. Not always willingly at first, but I finally get around to accepting change, especially if it is good.

Today I am happy, very happy. My spirit is lifted because I have come to terms with stuff and put a closure to certain things, like the loss of my 'boobs.'

And the happiness continues. This is what I call efficiency—a system that is working very well. I got a phone call. I am to see the plastic surgeon at St Thomas' on Monday. I was not expecting anything so soon—I guess when you don't expect anything from people, you can never be disappointed if things don't happen the way you wish them to. Also, when things do work out you become pleasantly surprised. On this occasion I am pleasantly surprised that the system is so quick. It's all good.

As much as I have enjoyed having space in which to think, one cannot delay the inevitable for too long. Things must happen. There has been a lot to take in. The biggest shock in all this is my sudden inability to plan for the future, another reason why my meeting with Mr Singh has left me feeling so accomplished. But no matter how many decisions I can make, at many times I simply have to go with the flow and take one day at a time. That is something I am so not used to. Having said that, you quickly learn life goes on. Nothing stops simply because you have been diagnosed with some type of cancer or the other. It is no longer a death sentence, so the best way to tackle this is 'grit your teeth and bear it.'

It is at times like this that I appreciate my Philosophy degree. I can, and am, drawing on the knowledge I have learnt along the way. Yet even though I know I have the inner strength to contend with difficulties, I pray I am able to show my vulnerability. As I am strong, so I am weak. I pray I do not hide my weakness. I know it will take more than cancer or any operation to destroy that strength. My strength cometh from the Lord who made Heaven and Earth. When the chips are down, I will lift up my eyes to the Lord. He will see me through my dark moments. More than everything else, His will be done. I am ready for whatever the good Lord has in store for me. He is my Father, the only thing that matters and the only thing that counts. I will not question Him in any manner, shape or from. I am all His and let Him do what He pleases with my life. On my part, I can only try.

It is truly amazing reading back at some of my entries before diagnosis. It's as though I have known all along that all has not been well, but I have not been listening. My subconscious has been talking to me, but I have not been listening. It took the wake-up call of this cancer to make me adjust. If only we listened more to ourselves and others.

When I hear how other people tackle their cancer, I cannot but feel some form of admiration for them. On the other hand, some people give in to the illness for personal reasons. In my opinion, if you have just lost everything, if you have lost a loved one, if you have had to make the necessary adjustments to pay bills and more bills, the dose of perspective that comes with cancer might just be a good thing. It allows you to focus on other things and appreciate life for what it is.

16 September

I have been in and out of the office, having to take time off for various hospital appointments. Not ideal, but it is what it is.

This day in the office has been productive. I got a lot done and frankly, it was a good distraction. We all need a structure in life to help to us remain focused.

I spoke with two of my colleagues in the office who happen to be battling with cancer. Rosemary was very helpful, coming up with some useful advice and websites for me to check out. The best piece of information I got was the Disability and Discrimination Act part—apparently cancer sufferers come under that group, counting as 'disabled' for having the diagnosis. It means that we cannot be discriminated against in employment, housing, or education because of our illness. I will check it out.

My boss left the company today. I was so sad. He has been one of my best line managers ever. I am going to miss him dearly, but he is moving on to a new and better position. To be honest, bidding him goodbye makes me think again what a shame it is that I have cancer, because if I was healthier I would also have been leaving for newer pastures. I could have really done with the salary increase. Never mind, I have a lot to be thankful for. I have to count my blessings and name them one by one. My present employers have not been bad to me at all, so I must not be an ingrate. In any event, since I am remaining at this job, I will miss my boss.

I have just read Danielle Steel's *Lightning*. In a big coincidence, it deals with breast cancer, and a woman who is struck by it just as she is trying to juggle husband, family and work at a prestigious law firm. Rather informative. I think I have already mentioned that I am in a fortunate but lonely position in that I do not have to deal with a boyfriend, partner or spouse. It is a weight off my shoulders, because it seems it would be just more source of stress that I could do without. What if the person is not able to come to terms with the diagnosis and the changes it brings, physically, mentally and emotionally? Surely there must be a shift in emphasis from being a partner, lover, friend to becoming a caregiver. I don't know what happens if that shift never happens, and I guess I may never know. I am thankful that I don't need to. At the end of the day, it is only the good Lord who is our lover, friend and comforter.

In Him I personally lay my trust and my hope. Yes, people can help. Yes, people will be there for you. But when you lay down at night with your private thoughts, only He knows how to comfort you. He will never leave you and will never, ever disappoint you. Life is an extraordinary journey. We can only wait to see how it will end—because it will definitely come to an end one day soon.

The only thing bugging me, and which will continue to bug me, is the attitude of some people. It's the judgemental way certain people obviously feel, the way they would clearly prefer me not to tell anyone about what is going on in my life because if I do, it will become widely known that I have cancer. I have to remain patient and tolerant when I hear stuff like that for a number of reasons. It is *my* cancer. I did not inflict the cancer on myself, of course, yet even I had, so what? It is good to talk. This illness is not a secret. I have not done anything wrong and definitely have nothing to be so ashamed of.

At the end of the day, it will be my choice, my decision who I tell and what I tell them. If I chose to talk about bilateral reconstruction, so be it. If I chose not to talk about anything, so be it. It is my choice and my choice alone. Let those who do not want me to talk about it wait until they have something they wish to talk about as strongly as I wish to talk about the cancer! Then it will be up to them to decide.

I guess it is a cultural thing. In West Africa, there are illnesses that are not talked about openly, because it is believed that by being sick the patient is settling some karma for their ancestors. It is believed that nothing happens without a reason. Thus, if you are ill, it may possibly be the result of someone cursing the living daylights out of you or your ancestors. No one is ill for being ill's sake. The gods or other supernatural powers always have something to do with it.

To me it seems like a way of not accepting responsibility, and perhaps another way of trying to apportion blame on something or someone else. Would I be wrong to call it an escape mechanism? A lot of Africans do not know how to deal with illnesses. It is kept quiet, not talked about in case your enemies might be lurking around, and dancing for joy that they are winning.

Though peculiar, it is a very strong belief system in West African culture that these illnesses are not natural. People hold many strong beliefs in the supernatural and evil forces—they are certain that they exist and are out there. And when people from this background hear about my illness and want me to keep quiet about it, they are trying to be helpful, or are scared that I have brought on some shame. But the shame is not mine, I wish they would understand. If one does not know what to say, then I suggest silence is an option. Silence, as they say, is golden.

I slept for a long time last night. I was exhausted. Then, as I said, today was quite productive—I guess a good night's rest goes a very long way. I also completed my course of antibiotics. Yippee! Generally things are looking up.

A couple of things are keeping me going, and occupying my thoughts with my upcoming surgery. Foremost is the thought that I am going to go for a breast reduction. Hilarious! Unfortunately, I will have to invest in new bras, but I will be able to get suitable ones. Can't wait.

This day is ending. My mind is tired and I am beginning to feel tired in body as well. Although that too could be psychological, who knows?

Sunday 17 September

Did not do my PLR2 assessment. Obviously, my motivation is beginning to wane. The spirit is willing, but the flesh is weak.

I have finished reading Danielle Steel's novel, *Lightning*. It was truly an eye opener. The description of the main character, Alex, being sick in the loo after chemotherapy confirmed my misgivings. The book made it so real that I could relate to it in an instant. There is absolutely no way I am taking chemotherapy now. No such luck. The bilateral reconstruction will have to do, end of discussion! If they cannot capture the cancer cells in that single operation, then forget it. I have absolutely no intention of having that stuff in my body.

If I knew then what I know now, I would not have bothered having the lump checked out. Sometimes ignorance is bliss, albeit no excuse. But why should I worry about excuses? It is my life and, pardon me, I can do with it as I may. No one can force me to have chemo, and I do not want it, so I will not be having it. Still, I suppose it's a good thing that right now I really don't give a toss how anyone feels about me. I can only feel for myself, and I will only do what is good for me.

The cancer diagnosis was a birthday present—icing on the cake. Is that not telling me something? I do not intend to please anyone but myself right now. I am the one who has to have treatment, so I can decide what treatment I do or do not want to have.

Thank goodness for the internet! At least I have spent some quality time this morning reading about reconstruction. None of it sounds (or reads) sexy, and sometimes I feel as dubious about the reconstruction as I do about chemo. The more I read about this, the more determined I am to opt out.

Monday 18 September

This journal is a lifeline. It is the only place I can pour out my emotions without being told how to feel, or how I should not feel. If I feel lousy, happy, numb, or vulnerable, I can write it all down in my journal.

Today I woke up at 4:00 a.m. and started thinking about my meeting with Mr Ross, the Plastic Surgeon at St Thomas'. I just want to listen to what he has to say and then put my point across: It is my cancer and my body that will have to go through the treatment. And while trying to remove cancer is one thing, having to live with the aftermath is another thing altogether. I must be able to reconcile the two. Whatever decision I make, I know that God will be guiding me. With that in mind, I am not scared in the slightest. Irritated, yes, but I am not fearful.

I have decided I will finally speak with a counsellor. I don't want to bottle up my emotions when I have the opportunity to let someone else listen to me without passing judgement. It will be such a relief to have someone paid to listen—not by me, either, because these sessions are all free of charge to patients. I am hoping it will do me some good.

Cancer patients are offered a lot of support in one form or another. At the Princess Royal Hospital, the Breast Cancer Unit has a counsellor assigned to patients. I had been told about the counsellor when I was initially diagnosed, but did not feel the need to take up the offer at that time. Of course, since then the cancer has not gone away, and now that I have a date for surgery it feels like a good time to speak with someone and try to fathom my roller coaster of thoughts and feelings.

Everyone has to embark upon some personal journey during their life. The time has come for one of mine. I know from experience these journeys can be lonely, although you may not be alone. You may be in the hearts and minds of friends and family, and they may be near you. But the journey must be one you take on your own. It is your personal experience, your story, the shoes will only fit you.

I will be taking this journey—a lonely walk to see the plastic surgeon today. I pray I do not cry. I feel strong, but it is a walk I would rather not have to make. I guess I will just have to take very slow, steady paces. I feel as though I am having an appointment with my executioner. Although I am well aware of the reason for it, that does not make the thought of a meeting on how an important part of my body will be reconstructed any easier. Even though my logical mind knows this is part of saving my life, my heart is crying and wishing I did not have to go through it. Rationally, I do not feel sorry for myself at all. Yet it is an inconvenience, to say the least. I cannot plan, and I am losing the desire to do anything else.

I digress, now and again, because my mind wanders, now and again. I forgive myself.

My meeting with Mr Ross went well. He saw me at the Plastic's outpatient unit. We agreed to have the surgery scheduled at St Thomas'. My breast surgeon and consultant, Mr Singh, will carry out the breast cancer surgery and then Mr Ross and his plastics team will continue with immediate reconstruction.

I had to obviously undress so he could have a look at my breasts and do a rough sketch of them. He asked me whether I would like to go up or down in size. I told him I would like to go down. I have been richly endowed with a pair of beautiful bosoms, but if I am on the path of reinventing myself, I really do not see the need of going any larger. Mr Ross found that a novelty, as he says most individuals ask for a breast increase.

He also advised me that I could not go too small, either, as it would be disproportionate to my bone structure. We settled for a reasonable size that would not be disproportionate. He was so caring and considerate, and educated me when I had questions.

I asked about my nipples and whether he would fix them back at the same time. He found it amusing in a nice way, and told me that I cannot have everything at once. He said my nipples would have to be discarded because they were cancerous. That had not crossed my mind. So I've learned something new today.

We also discussed where the muscles would be taken from to recreate my new boobs. Muscle could be taken from the back, buttocks or stomach, each having its pros and cons. In my case, muscle was going to be taken from my stomach. Although I only just had any to spare, as I had lost quite a lot of weight. In simple terms, I was going to have a tummy tuck.

During that meeting he got out his diary and booked the date for the surgery: October 5. That's barely two weeks away. Mr Ross made it very clear to me that as a cancer patient, my surgery was a priority, as it was a life-or-death situation. He was very knowledgeable, kind and considerate in all that he said and the way he said it.

At the end of the meeting, I left knowing that I would be entering the hospital for surgery on 4 October, plus I knew I would not be having my original nipples replaced. I knew that the breast consultant would be coming to St Thomas' to do the surgery for the double mastectomy (full), and the plastics surgeons would be carrying out the bilateral reconstruction immediately afterwards.

I went for the consultation all by myself, and felt it was a lot to take in all at once. Despite Mr Ross' consideration, at the end of it I just felt frustrated with the situation. This can't be taken care of and put behind me soon enough.

23 September

I went with Auntie Roli for my pre-admission assessment at St Thomas'. The pre-admission assessment is normally done a week before surgery. It is to ascertain that I am in good health (besides the obvious). My weight, height, and BMI were taken to help the surgery team, including the anaesthetist, prepare. Things went smoothly. I had my blood taken again. That was to make sure my blood group is known in the event that I need a blood transfusion during surgery. It was a routine procedure and is meant to save time on the actual day of admission.

Work is hectic. I am trying my best possible to tidy up loose ends. I can only do so much, and so the rest will simply have to be dealt with by someone else in the team.

My weight is dropping off fast, I guess from the stress and worry of not knowing.

Cancer has been a Pandora's Box full of surprises. The biggest surprise is how easy it is to misjudge friendship. Cancer has shown me who my friends are, and what finer stuff some people are made of. Some people you think are your friends are really not, while others you think don't care about you really do. For some friends, it is a chore to just pick up the phone and to say hello.

I have been told that *despite my condition, the world does not revolve around me.* How insensitive could a person be at a time like that? But the good thing about such friends, and the beauty of friendship, is that you do not have to keep them.

However, a really good friend will always have a fair-sized cemetery in which to bury the faults of another true friend. The beauty of being human is that we are all entitled to our opinions. We are all able to pass judgement about each other, rightly or wrongly.

I digress, I know. I just wish I knew how to slow down. I don't know how to do that, although I am positive I am going to learn the hard way. I went to college last Wednesday, the hospital on Monday, and for now I am still working full time. No wonder my mind is rushing around everywhere, too.

Let me say, let us thank God for family. I guess we all take family for granted. Then a crisis like this strikes, and all of a sudden one begins to appreciate why God has created the family. There are times when we need things to be done with no obligations or conditions attached. The only group of people who do that are the ones known as 'family.' To Mama, Thelma, Sam, Dukuye, Ayulie, Demi, Auntie Roli, Uncle Godfrey, and Jnr, my family, I thank you all.

26 September

I had a wonderful afternoon with one of my dear friends, Foster. He took me out for lunch, where we were able to talk freely. We reminisced about our time in University together while we were both studying for our Law Degrees. During our time at University, we both had personal challenges to contend with. Mine was Ayulie's health, and I had to nurse my son while holding down a full time job and studying part time. In my second year, I had a major operation to contend with. But all in all, I got through my challenges, and Foster got through his.

I reminded him of how I was recuperating from major surgery and had missed my lectures, but I still had an assignment to hand in. I had asked Foster to provide me with the bullet points for me to write the assessment. The way he broke it down was amazing. Needless to say, I passed the assessment, and without having to spend hours and hours trying to fathom it out.

I talked about my feelings towards the upcoming surgery, the whole illness, and how I had to give up not taking a job offer. What Foster did today was put things into perspective. His words remind me of what I have already been through, and that what is happening now is merely a challenge that I can and will overcome, no matter what. His words were all it took to remind me not to doubt myself. He told me he has the uttermost faith in me, and I should not be scared to make my own decisions and do what I need to do.

At times like this, one is grateful to have a very good friend who understands. It also helps to remember we have both had our fair share of difficulties. From most of them, we have come out victorious.

What is happening to me is simply another challenge, another trial. To a certain extent, it is up to me to ensure I come out victorious. Where I fall short, I will pray and remain hopeful. And most importantly of all, by talking to me about past trails we have overcome, and how much we've each accomplished since then, Foster has reminded me that I will have a life after cancer.

28 September
The day is drawing nigh. D-day is fast approaching.

I returned to work yesterday after two interesting days off. I had to take Ayulie to Guy's and St Thomas' to deal with his own food challenge. We must hope this challenge soon becomes a thing of the past, so that he is able to once again eat a wide variety of healthy foods. The restrictive diet he is on because of his food intolerances is unsustainable, especially when he gets older and begins to socialise much more with his peers. After all, sharing meals, trying out different tastes and textures of foods, and drinking with family and friends is a big part of socializing. While it is one thing to avoid certain foods out of personal choice, being hesitant to eat because you might have a reaction to the food is another thing entirely, and makes one very self-conscious.

I cannot begin to explain how important and how significant my son has been in my cancer journey.

First, I have to tell you about Ayulie for you to understand.

Ayulie was born by caesarean section in a London hospital. He weighed in at a healthy 8 lbs, 10 oz. I had slight complications. My waters had broken, but after 48 hours I had still not given birth. I had no labour pains; I had to be induced, but no joy. The baby was in distress so there was no other option left but to have him by c-section. Ayulie was taken to intensive care unit for observation. The first time I met my son was through a picture taken when he was born.

He was given to me after 24 hours. Looking back, I really don't know how I coped. When I met him face-to-face I was so happy, my heart was bursting. That was my son, my very own flesh and blood.

I was never into babies and my son was the first baby I held without being scared. Babies have always seemed too fragile for me; all they do is cry or sleep. Not my cup of tea, babies—until I had my own.

He was absolutely adorable. Like all newly born babies, he was a joy to behold. His father and I loved our bundle of joy. I remember the first time his father came to the hospital to meet his son. He walked in proudly carrying a bunch of flowers for me. He had such a big grin on his face. It was a nice to see. He also bought me a tri-colour necklace and bracelet set for the birth of his son. Thoughtful gestures.

My son and I were both discharged from hospital after seven days. All was well at home. I breast fed Ayulie for four months, after which time I had to return to work. At this stage also I had become a single parent. The father of my son and I simply wanted different things. I was very happy to have a baby, but was not sure I could live with his father for the rest of my life. Also, we were younger so our tolerance threshold for things one would now overlook did not exist at the time, to say nothing of silly things that may have been said out of youthful exuberance. Meanwhile, Ayulie and I were a package deal. Ayulie's father made his choice and I made mine, and from that day when Ayulie was four months old, I have been a single parent with sole responsibility for the upkeep of my son.

I had a return date to work, so I made a conscious decision that I was not going to mix breast-feeding with formula milk. Instead I stopped breast-feeding and put Ayulie on Cow and Gate formula milk.

It turned out that the Cow and Gate formula was not good for Ayulie. He suffered severe allergic reactions, to the point that he was unable to keep any of the milk down. His skin and hair also suffered.

From these effects, we spent the next seven years in and out of hospital. My son was not growing, he was unable to eat, and he reacted to virtually everything he put in his mouth. He had trouble breathing; he was wheezing all the time. My poor son! It was so hard seeing a child in such distress.

Ayulie starting taking Soya milk as a substitute, but has remained allergic to all dairy products, wheat gluten, additives and preservatives. This makes his diet limited.

And so seven years ago I became a caretaker even more than a mother. My four-month-old child changed from a healthy baby to a troubled and unhealthy baby. I blamed myself for this, and said that God was punishing me for becoming a single mother. For two years I could not shake away the feeling of loathing I had for myself. And no one prepared me for what I would face over the next seven years. There are no textbooks I could refer to, no template for the agony a mother faces seeing her child in pain.

I will not bore you with the whole story of the seven long years I went through nursing my son to good health. But I will narrate some of the poignant moments

Ayulie started nursery when he was four months old. Luckily, I found a nursery right opposite the office I worked. The nursery members of staff were given strict instructions not to add butter or milk to his mashed potatoes, which were freshly made. But on particular day I was called at work to be told Ayulie was unwell. A staff member had added some butter to his mashed potato because she felt they were too bland otherwise. Ayulie's reaction—he was only two years old at the time—was severe. He could not keep anything down, and became so dehydrated that he shed a layer of skin. I took him home and had to call an ambulance. From one lunch at the nursery, he spent the next week in hospital. I would go to the hospital after work, leave the hospital at 4:00 a.m. after giving Ayulie his bath and return at 5:00 p.m. I slept in the hospital beside my son. At the end of that week, I had lost a stone in weight and collapsed in the hospital.

On another occasion, I rushed him to hospital because he had an asthma attack. He was put on a nebulizer. I cannot recount how many times we spent in Children's A & E, how many times he was admitted in hospital, how many times I would get to work and, before I could sit down, get the dreaded phone call that he was unwell.

A couple of things happened during this period. I was a shy, retiring person. I would rather not confront an issue, indeed, I would go and bury myself in the sand rather than engage in an argument. I used to want everything to just go away.

When I had Ayulie and became his carer, I quickly realised I had to also become my child's advocate. He was my responsibility. I had to speak up and had to speak for him. Over the next seven years, my voice became stronger and louder. I would be heard—because it was not just myself being heard, it was my son who had to be heard through me. I was not going to let anyone or anything stop me from speaking on his behalf.

So by default, I became a voice. And it is the voice I first used for Ayulie that I used for myself on my cancer journey.

Ayulie's growth was, for obvious reasons, becoming slower. He was assigned a speech therapist, as well as a food psychologist to help him, as he had become petrified of food and eating. I had to see the speech therapist and food psychologist during their office hours—which, being regular hours, were also my office hours. At the time I worked for a Housing Association, with one of the meanest bosses in the whole wide world. Just evil personified. But sometimes evil is good to have in your life. Evil strengthens you, and gives you resolve that good will triumph no matter what.

The speech therapist was sympathetic and agreed to have meetings with me at my place of work. My line manager did not like that. I was a junior member of staff, having such meetings at work. How very dare I?

When Ayulie was five, a consultant paediatrician asked me how on earth I had been able to hold down a full-time job and look after my son. She also said that in order to help us, she would admit him for a week to test all his allergies.

At the end of the week, we were nowhere nearer in getting to grips with his allergies because he had reactions to almost everything. But her kindness and understanding were to be applauded.

She had no understanding or comprehension of the world I was living in. All I knew then was I was a carer and had to work. I had to hold down my job even it killed me. I did not want to be on welfare. I had a job, how could I give my job up? The irony of it was I was good at the job that I did. No one ever faulted my work. I was young and did not realize how much evil and lack of compassion was out there in the world.

I juggled my work with my son's illness because I had no other choice. The only reason I was able to hold down a job is because I had to stay in a junior role. I applied for jobs to be promoted but was not given a look. I trained people into roles that I applied for, but was not even short-listed myself.

Something had to give. My son was far more important than moving, being promoted.

My boss started taking down notes as to when I got to work and what I was doing. The bottom line is, she had started discriminating. I spoke to a few more experienced people in the workplace and they simply told me she was discriminating against me and I should join the Union. I joined Union, and from being an ordinary member I rose to become a shop steward, where I started representing other members of staff who were being treated unfairly.

Ayulie also led to my studying Law. I already had a degree in Philosophy. But that on its own was not going to help me. As his mother, I was never, ever going to allow anyone treat him unfairly. I needed to know and understand my rights. I needed to know I could speak clearly. I needed to know I could represent my son. I just needed to know. And so I empowered myself.

I grew stronger and more knowledgeable as a person during my years as a carer and advocate.

And I also learned then that all illnesses have a spiritual journey as well as a physical and emotional one.

I will never forget another trip to the hospital. I had been sitting with Ayulie, just looking at him, who was looking so poorly. We were waiting for the ambulance. I was praying, and I said to God, 'Dear God, you can have him now, I release him into your care, because his suffering is too much.' I begged God to take him if it would release him. There is only so much pain a human being should be allowed to go through. At the same time I said those prayers, I felt the angel of the Lord touch my shoulders and take the burden off me. It felt like a physical manifestation of the Lord. I could feel someone take something off my shoulders.

I am only narrating what happened.

If I had not believed in miracles before, that day I did. Because from that day, Ayulie's health started improving and he began to get stronger.

As Ayulie started growing older, he began to have his own voice. He had a beautiful voice; he was a caring, intuitive child. He shared and gave away all his food to his friends at school, for obvious reasons. But there were times my heart cried seeing him struggle to be included at meal times. He would put a sandwich on his plate, knowing he could not eat it, with salted crisps, which he could eat. He learnt how to starve himself all day at school and eat only when he got home. He cared about others and was just a joy to behold.

Even now, he has reactions to many foods, but he has come far and is able to cope with his asthma and food choices.

So this July, when my son said to me, 'Mum,' with tears in his eyes about a dream he had, God was speaking to Him to speak to his mum.

I truly believe I have got the strength to deal with my cancer journey because of what I learned when I nurtured my son back to relatively good health. Meanwhile, after our appointment at Guy's and St Thomas' today, I can only hope his health continues improving.

As for mine... Today I felt very angry with my ailment. It is as though it is being imposed upon me, and I do not have a choice even about the treatment. I cannot even begin to accept this idea that the 'tummy tuck' and 'new boobs' are something I should be looking forward to. I have no complaints about the way I look now. At least if I don't like how I currently look, I can exercise or restrict my calorie intake and modify my body that way. If not for cancer, none of this invasive surgery would be necessary.

The highlights of my days are when my friends call me and, with their talk and kindness, let me know a cancer diagnosis does not stop one from enjoying oneself. It has been welcoming to get invitations to have some fun before treatment. My talk with Foster was so comforting, and I've also enjoyed some small dinner parties, drinks, etc. My friends have been putting a smile on my face.

2 October

Today I attended a conference on current Leasehold reform legislation at Tottenham Court Road.' After the conference I walked up to Charing Cross station to meet up with my dear friend Daniel for a drink. I walked slowly, taking in all the sites and appreciating nature. The buildings, the hustle and bustle of Londoners going about their business, lots and lots of shops, black cabs, Trafalgar Square—I guess I was taking it all in because a part of me realised I may never see this ever again. After all, I have no clue what the outcome of my surgery was going to be. Tomorrow is promised to no one.

All of a sudden I realised how beautiful London is. I viewed the environment as a tourist, appreciating little things. As one who lives and works in London, I think I had taken the beauty and what it has to offer for granted. Really seeing it today was refreshing and therapeutic.

A lot has happened since the end of last week. This past Friday was my last day at work for a while. My goodness, it was terribly busy, with many meetings, and in between it was emotional. I was advised of the changes that have been or will be made, and met the temp who would be covering my position in my absence.

The highlight of the day was the most beautiful bouquet of exotic flowers which I received from my colleagues. It was such a sweet gesture. What I loved the most was the teddy bear that came with the bouquet, which I will be taking to hospital with me.

It felt really strange tidying up my desk. I was not going on holiday, and I was not changing jobs. I was tidying my desk to go on what they call 'sick leave,' when in all honestly I did not feel unwell in the slightest. Life is strange.

My departure was so emotional, I wept in the lift all the way to my car. Driving through my tears, I got home safely.

On getting home, I took Jnr and Ayulie to Thelma's place, where they would be staying for the weekend. With them settled elsewhere, I had contemplated going on a two-day retreat to prepare my mind, body, and soul for the adventure ahead. The life of a single parent normally means no time to feel sorry for yourself or indulge. Things have to get done, whether one likes it or not. This was a chance to take a break from it, with my boys seen to. There was a convent I had been looking at, with Auntie's encouragement, where I could rest, think, and pray.

Yet, as one has the right to change one's mind, I spoke to a friend who was unsure that going for a retreat would be ideal. I tried to explain why I wanted to isolate myself from the rest of the world, when I really felt like being surrounded by people. Truly, once I looked twice I did not think it was a very clever idea to spend the last 48 hours on my own with my own thoughts. On the brink of surgery, I was not really in the mood to go to dark places or to have dark thoughts in a convent.

So between us, we decided the retreat was not such a good idea. Oh dear, I had to break the news to my Auntie, who had already spoken to the reverend Sisters.

Instead, this evening I opted to go with a long-time friend who took me out for dinner. I happen to have a good number of friends from childhood and from school through university. At this time, my friends from everywhere have started coming out of the woodwork. I have often thought that it seems that one advantage of being single is that you do not have to answer to anyone. And even so, even when you are single, you will have help—even if friends only help because they know you do not have a significant other.

My dear friend took me out to eat, knew the right things to say and the right things to do. He led and all I had to do was follow. And he had gone out of the way to make it a lovely evening, because of the circumstances. It was surreal, even magical and mystical, and absolutely beautiful. When you are faced with a life or death situation not knowing what the outcome will be, all of a sudden from nowhere the world becomes a more beautiful place. I think I've found joy and beauty in everything and everyone. I see the beauty in everything, no matter how simple. I am grateful for everything. All these kind gestures seem extraordinary. I wished the evening did not have to end. He also gave me a couple of gifts to cheer me up before I left, another thoughtful gesture. The evening will always be etched in my memory. The icing on the cake was an open invitation to Lusaka, all expenses paid, if I survived the challenge ahead. Hmm—that will be something for me to consider.

Things got better over this weekend. Josef had a small dinner party in my honour, another thoughtful gesture. It was relaxing. Toritseju (TJ), Chudi, and Josef's friend, Annie, joined us over wine, pasta, steak, chicken, prawns and vegetables. For the first time in a very long while, I actually ate and drank properly. Josef ended the evening by giving me a parfum and a bottle of wine. I am really being spoilt, and boy oh boy, I am enjoying it.

Gbadero came to see me on Sunday with her son. We had a good chat. At the end of it I dropped her off at Brixton and did some shopping while I was there, buying fish, chicken and other bits and pieces for Jnr and Ayulie. It seems as though I have so much to do and yet so little time to do it. I want to study, but cannot.

Gbadero also gave me £100 towards a pair of silk pyjamas, because I have read that my 'boobs' will be sensitive after surgery. An article in a magazine talked about a lady who had a mastectomy, and it said that silk was a nice, gentle fabric for the skin after surgery. I grasped onto her experience and decided I could use some silk pyjamas of my own.

George, a professional and personal friend of mine, rang. He is such a joy to speak with; he always puts a smile on my face and at the same time he is sensitive. He has a wicked sense of humour, and can make light of every situation without taking away from the gravity or complexity of what is happening. He is as thoughtful as he is hopeful and inspiring.

I went to my hair dresser, Doris, to get my hair braided in cornrows. I'm not sure I like it, but it is convenient, or let's say, it will do the job. I will not have to fuss and worry about my hair with everything else going on, but I will still look presentable.

Overall I was feeling very tearful today. Guess it comes with the territory.

***

My dear friend and reader, you have now read the first part of my journal. You have seen my daily thoughts surrounding my cancer diagnosis, the mental and emotional turmoil it put me through. The highs and lows.

The generosity of family, friends and colleagues.

The knowledge that every day is different from the last.

If you continue reading, my dearest friend, you will learn about the treatment and the joys of having family and friends. About meeting people who have empathy, who are sensitive and caring.

I met you for the second time during my treatment phase.

I salute each and every person who has walked with me, cried for me and with me, laughed at me and with me. Everyone who has encouraged me and let me know there is life beyond a cancer diagnosis.

I would call myself a rather private person. I do not particularly enjoy sharing my trials and tribulations with too many people. For many years, I sought solace and strength in reading self-help books, motivational books, books that inspire, books that teach about leadership and life lessons. I read lots of fiction and nonfiction. Books have helped shape my life, and formed me into the person I am today.

During my avid reading, I came across Susan Jeffers' book, Feel the Fear and Do It Anyway.

The way she touched on the fear we all have in us was an eye-opener. I was struck by how she empathised that it was one thing to feel the fear, and another to let it stop you from doing something.

The book has proved very helpful, because although I had made the decision to have surgery, I was naturally scared. My mind was scared and playing havoc with me. But I was not going to back out at the last minute.

And so, to quote Susan Jeffers: feel the fear, but do it anyway.

PHASE TWO: TREATMENT

3 October

How do you prepare yourself for something like this? I do not have the answers. I lack the skills and tools. It is new terrain. I have not walked on this path ever before. There is a lot to take on board, and it is emotionally draining to have to cope with it. Especially while people want to believe you are solving problems by undergoing these trials.

I have tried to prepare myself for the journey ahead, but there is only so much I can do. Now I need to rest and leave it in the hands of the Almighty Lord. He gave me the ailment for a reason, and I hope that one day I will be able to fathom why. Until then, I feel at peace with myself and the world despite my problems.

I went shopping today, or perhaps I should say I went for some retail therapy. For the very first time in my life, I actually understand what that phrase means. It was nice buying stuff—especially things that were different, things that I would never have bought under normal circumstances. Silk pyjamas and silk blouses, which I know I will need in hospital and at home after surgery. Great stuff.

It has left me feeling tired, but happy.

4 October

The day we have all been waiting for. I had a lousy night. Sleep eluded me. I woke up at three in the morning and could not get back to sleep. Figuring I should be useful, I brought out chicken from the freezer to defrost. Around 4:00 a.m. I finally drifted off to sleep again, and I woke up for good at 6:30 a.m.

I decided to go for my counselling session at Princess Royal. At first I wasn't sure—really, I did not want to talk for someone just to listen to my problems. The counsellor assigned to the cancer unit is a listening one—I talked to her for an hour, and she did not offer any opinion whatsoever, just an ear.

I did not feel like driving. The brisk walk to the hospital from Orpington station—approximately two and a half miles each way—was refreshing and helped to clear my head. The road leading from the station to the hospital is in a suburban area, with lots of green space, trees and woodlands. It was very peaceful, and the walk allowed me time to be at one with myself and nature. I did not think too much of anything, but just embraced the cool breeze and scenery.

When I got home from the counselling, I cooked rice and stew for Jnr and Ayulie. Mother came over. According to my instructions, I rang the hospital to find out if they had a bed for me. I was told there was no bed, but I should come anyway. I had already packed my things, so my mother and I took the train to St Thomas'.

When I arrived I had to speak with Mr Robin, registrar of
Mr Ross Plastic Consultant, SHO. There was also a visiting surgeon from Switzerland who was going to be an observer. I was advised by Mr Robin that my breast surgeon from Princess Royal would be arriving in the morning to remove the tumour, after which the plastic surgeons will carry out the reconstruction immediately.

I was informed my notes were missing, but they carried on with my assessment regardless. This did mean I had to go for yet more blood tests. My white blood cells were low, but I could not feel bothered by that at this stage.

As for the Plastics Team at St Thomas'—OMG! And hello! They were like Hollywood legends: extremely good looking, well dressed, well spoken. Walking adverts for cosmetic surgery. They all looked like Greek gods. This definitely boosted my confidence in their abilities.

It might seem odd to notice how well-dressed one's surgeons are before surgery. And, well, they did have on good suits, designer glasses. They had wonderful faces. And admiring them was definitely an excellent distraction from what I am about to face. Noticing silly details makes the situation lighter, and makes one realise that one is, after all, still human. It was a good distraction just to admire the handsome, professional people around me. Thinking about the surgery would have been a sheer nightmare. And there is seriously not much else to think about in hospital, where you are surrounded by others with their own troubles. It is surprising where we dig deep in order to survive. Yes, I admit my thoughts may have been superficial in this case, but as Alexander Pope says, 'a thing of beauty is a joy forever.' And admiring it was proof that I was still breathing.

But eye candy aside, their professionalism, their disposition, and a subtle but present seriousness were impressive. They knew I was there for reconstructive surgery and furthermore, they would do their best to save my life. Their customer relations skills were the best I have ever seen. During my assessment, they marked out the areas on my 'boobs' where they would operate, as well as drawing a rough sketch for their own purposes. They showed a lot of sensitivity during this time. I obviously had to undress for them to do it, but they were so professional and friendly that it put me at ease. Their sensitivity and empathy further touched me.

They also explained to me what they were going to do and how they were going to go about it. They told me what time the operation would start and what to expect. I was having a double mastectomy and immediate bilateral reconstruction using my tummy muscles, otherwise known as a 'tram flap.' They reminded me that it is very important that the markings they had made remain there so that they don't get it wrong.

They also asked if I had any questions, and whether I understood the surgery that I was about to undergo. I asked them to distinguish between cosmetic surgery and reconstructive surgery. I was told that reconstructive surgery is all about repairing and restoring someone's body, which makes it a necessity, while cosmetic surgery is used to change a person's appearance in a way that makes it desirable, but not always essential.

I was also told all the things that could go wrong with the surgery, including side effects. Like my bowels would be affected, and other risks. They asked if I knew what I was doing and had me sign the consent form. Finally, they left me with the parting words, 'You will be having one of the most complicated procedures in plastic surgery.'

My parting words in reply were, 'Let me look better on my way out than on my way in!' I also asked them to please come with steady hands to carry out the procedure the next day.

It is wonderful how words just come to you. I hadn't planned to say anything like that joke, the words flowed. I was calm, and overall I felt much better when I saw the team who would operate on me.

The Plastics team left me more hopeful and relaxed than I felt before meeting them.

When they finally finished, they thanked me for the way I dealt with the questions and examination. They went further to say my positive outlook and attitude has also given them the confidence to carry out the surgery. NHS any time, any day for me.

While I was being prepared for surgery, my mother was in the visitor's waiting room. Up until now she had been alone. Yet she was not alone for much longer, as Teju, Toritseju Thelma, Demi Ayulie and Jnr all turned up. They had all come straight from work or school to the hospital. We really had a full house in the waiting room! At around 8:00 p.m., I was taken to the hotel annexed to the hospital, as I still did not have a bed.

So we all moved over to the hotel. Although it was in the grounds of St Thomas' Hospital, it seemed like a proper hotel. I had my own self-contained room with a single bed, and best of all, I could have as many guests over as I liked. I lay down, and they either sat down or stood. We chatted late into the night. At 10:00, everyone left and I was alone in the hotel room with my thoughts and my thoughts. The surgery is scheduled for 8 o'clock the next morning.

I had a little book of hope to read, given to me by TJ's spouse. It was cute, and I read it from cover to cover. I simply could not sleep. I asked myself, *Why should I sleep? I will be sleeping throughout the procedure, so why waste time sleeping now?*

It was a long, long night. I don't know how I got through it.

5 October

Surgery day. Can you believe, I still do not have a hospital bed? I was taken to the private suite in the NHS, because even though there is no bed available for me in the general ward the surgery is still going to go ahead. The private room is comfortable, though. Very nice. Then I prepared for the surgery, putting on the hospital gown and white long socks.

Auntie Roli and Thelma were already there with me, even though it was just past 6:00 a.m. It must be horrible to see a family member being prepared for surgery. They did not show any fear or anguish at the time, at least not that I noticed, but I have been told that Auntie Roli was crying when I was finally wheeled to the theatre room.

The surgeons came again to check me out, making sure the markings were all intact. They told me they would see me later.

I remember just being there. It was a kind of out of body experience. I knew all this was taking place, but I was numb.

At last the porter came for me. Auntie Roli and Thelma escorted me to the theatre room, where were had to part. I am wheeled in. I would not see them, nor they me, until the end of the surgery. I cannot recall if I cried.

Thelma tells me that I said, 'It is okay if I don't make it.' She says at that point she knew I would pull through.

I draw a blank when I try to recall the next 13 hours. Surgery stated around 8:00 a.m. I was out of the theatre at around 9:00 that evening.

I hear that after eight hours, my mother stated losing the plot, crying and asking for her daughter. Bless her.

We all forgot one thing: reconstructive surgery for one breast is approximately eight hours. By simple addition, doing it twice should have been sixteen hours. Considering that, the surgeons did a good job and did it in very good time.

During the surgery, along with my breast tissue I also had 17 lymph nodes removed from my right arm. I believe the breast surgeon had no choice but to take them out to investigate and check that my cancer—which, as I mentioned, was at stage 3—has not spread to other parts of my body.

At some point during the day, a hospital bed must have been found, as I was given a room with three others in the

Alan Apley ward at noon on Friday, 6 October. Here I have a picturesque view of the houses of Parliament.

I salute the surgeons and team that saved my life. I thank you.

For Mama, Auntie Roli and Thelma, I apologise for the having to put you through all the waiting and uncertainty, but thank you for hanging in there. It must have been a very long day. I have witnessed my son being ill, even being admitted in hospital, but I have never had to accompany anyone that I know for surgery and wait and wait and wait for the outcome. It may happen one day, where I will be the one seeing someone go in for surgery and waiting for that person to come out. But unless or until it does, I will never understand how it feels to wait and wait and wait.

10 October

In the words of Bette Midler, is the heart afraid of breaking? Is the dream afraid of waking that never takes the chance?

Well, I have taken my chance.

My surgery was on 5 October, but I have only been able to write about the events now.

Thelma and I agreed that I would not have any visitors until Saturday, giving me at least 48 hours to regain some energy.

Of course, I could not remember anything of my 13-hour long surgery on Thursday apart from waking up in the recovery room, the place where they put you after surgery to revive from general anaesthetic. Mama was there when I woke up, sitting next to me. It was nice to have family around. I was too drowsy to remember anything they said, but I do remember vividly how, when she was leaving, she kissed her fingers and put them on my head.

The next day was uneventful. I only remember feeling sick and constantly wanting to throw up. Awful feeling, to say the least, and not something I really want to remember.

I remember having a bed bath whilst in recovery in Alan Apley ward. Ayulie, Demi, Jnr and Dukuye came to see me. Mama, Auntie Roli and Thelma were also there. It was great to see them all.

I was not a pretty sight to behold. I had a tubes coming out from so many places—I think I had a total of six tubes. The surgery itself had been successful, taking muscles from around my stomach to reconstruct my breasts. The only way I can explain it is that my tummy was sliced in half, from one hip to the other.

My recreated boobs look like eggs sunny side up. When I woke, where each nipple had been was instead a circle and a blue thread. Apparently the thread was there to enable the team to monitor blood vessels and ensure blood was flowing to my chest. Clever stuff, I must say. The scars are under the boobs and on both sides of my chest.

I was told in plain English that I have been rewired so that the blood vessels could get to my boobs. My belly button had been repositioned. To be honest, I did not have a clue what to expect, so the jury is still out. I've been totally indifferent with regards to how my boobs look at this point. I've certainly never had a boob job in my life, nor do I know anyone who has. It was difficult to figure out what the results might be like. Emotions like surprise are being kept in a separate compartment, to be opened at a later date.

The day after surgery, around 8:00 p.m., a Registrar was doing her rounds. For some reason, she looked at my eyes and realised my eyeballs were whiter than normal. I had several other doctors check up on me, but she was the first one to look at my eyes. She was of Asian descent, and that may have something to do with it—there are certain things that people of different cultures are more aware of. For dark-skinned people, certain symptoms are not as apparent. And by looking at the whites of my eyes, she spotted something crucial. She said I had lost too much blood. Along with the blood loss, my right arm was retaining too much fluid. So I had to be taken down for a two hour emergency surgery for what one could call minor complications.

It was not fun being rushed off with my sons, niece and brother looking on.

All I can remember is seeing tears rolling down their faces. I think the sight of me in an oxygen mask was a bit too much for my son and Dukuye.

By Saturday, I had many visitors. I am going to write down some of their names.

The first person to be at my bedside was my good friend Mr John Wiltshire. He travelled all the way from Redhill in Surrey to be there at 2:00 p.m. on the dot, when visiting time begins.

Then came:
Vigey, Paul.
Angela, Margaret
(both colleagues from the office)
Kenneth, Ayulie, Demi, Thelma, Auntie Roli, Jnr, Sam. On Sunday, I had many visitors as well—family and other friends.

I was drowsy for most of the time, so although I appreciate these visits I cannot remember much more about them. Although you think you remember everyone, it is obvious that memory fails when you are coming through the general anaesthetic agents. It takes a while for those to come out of your system. I ought to have opened a visitor's book.

12 October

I cannot recall much of what has happened in the last couple of days. Here are some of the highlights: mobilising, that is walking, unaided; having three drains out of five removed.

And how on earth could I forget to write about having a shower on Tuesday? Water all over my body, OMG, it was refreshing! Absolute joy. I have also been sleeping well, but not eating too much. I just do not have any appetite.

Tuesday was an emotional and spiritual low day, when I could not help but ponder and question. My situation was simply not making any sense to me. The pain was excruciating. My diagnosis, the surgery, all seemed surreal, but they were happening, had happened. I suppose some psychologists would say I am still in denial. Denial could be seen as a good thing. It suits me perfectly well, because if this is a dream I will wake up from it. What I still don't understand is why I am unable to identify with what is going on around me.

It seems as though someone pressed a pause or else a fast forward button on my life and I am watching it, simply staring as if at the television screen. Another puzzle that baffles me is my total lack of emotion. I feel devoid of emotions right now. I feel as though I am disconnecting and observing from a distance. I hope this is normal. I don't know what normal is anymore. Presumably this numbness, this emotional anaesthetic, is my way of surviving?

One day I am going to look back at this experience and understand the lessons that I ought to be learning. Right now I guess it would be wise not to look for anything to learn, as it would be more useful to concentrate on healing properly.

Wednesday was interesting. For the first time I spoke with a BBC 1 researcher who was looking for human interest stories in the hospital. These stories are meant to inspire and help those who watch them overcome adversity. I told him mine, and my story was covered by the BBC 1 hospital programme, City Hospital. I vividly remember telling the interviewer how important it is to keep a journal. But more on that later.

13 October

Oh dear, I must not forget to record my worst constipation nightmare. I have never been so constipated in my entire life! Among the many things this cancer journey has taught me, it has given me a new respect for 'excreta'—known to us a 'pooh' or 'shit.' When a body is healthy and works well, we take so little notice of these things. Not so for me any longer.

Well, it started on Friday 13, by which time my bowels had not opened for eight days. Of course, I thought that was okay, and that when the time was right my bowels would move by themselves. Are you kidding me? I had to wonder that as my bowel began to take a life of its very own. Yep, its very own. I drank litres of water and had been doing so since the operation. This means at least being dehydrated was not an issue. I had been eating, albeit in small quantities, but I think I had a substantial amount of food in me over the eight day period to ensure that my bowels opened properly. I wished!

I ate ground rice and vegetable soup—steamed, cooked soft dough made of rice flour, a West African dish that my friend Vigey brought —hoping that would assist my very important bowels. Nope, no show. We finally had to resort to taking laxatives. No joy. When that didn't work, we took the next step, moving on to suppositories—also no joy.

By this time, my bowels had taken over my entire body. I began to feel feverish and was experiencing plenty of discomfort. The only way I can describe it is like being in labour. I was beyond myself. I made several aborted attempts to move my bowels but only ended up straining my delicate area. There was even an attempt to use my fingers (obviously with gloves) to aid the culprit out of my bowels. Well, that was a fruitless attempt! Eventually I was given an enema. Beforehand, I was told I would be given a commode chair—something you have to sit on in the confines of your bed space, because you will not be in any position to 'dash' to the toilet when you finally have to go. Oh, my goodness. I had not seen the modern commode chair. I still had this ghastly image of a small bed pan. How was I to know that even commode chairs had gone revolutionary? Anyway, I was given a commode chair that looked very dignified with a cover. That made me feel better. I was still apprehensive about doing a 'pooh' in the ward, with other patients having to put up with the smell and noises that may emanate from my body. That was something I could not get my head around.

Having thought about all it, I aired my concerns to a lovely student nurse, Barry, who turned doing a 'pooh' into a dignified art form. He reminded me that people paid thousands of pounds to have colonic irrigation, and 'we all "shit,"' as he whispered to me quietly. That made me feel better about doing my long awaited 'pooh' when the time came. The enema was finally inserted into my being. The staff nurse was also magnificent, and along with Barry helped me retain my dignity. Once the enema was inserted, the time finally arrived. I made the dash to my distinguished commode. However, nothing happened there. The nurse came and rubbed my back, my goodness, bless her. The smell was not pleasant. The nurse left. I must have sat there for all eternity while nothing happened. I could not take it anymore so I dragged myself to a proper toilet, but to no avail. Then I got myself back to bed, where I did not have to wait long. The time came again, and this was not a false alarm. I made a mad dash to the commode and the heavens opened. Yippee! And when I say opened, I mean opened. Everything that I had in my body over the past eight days gushed out. I felt so bad for the poor patients sharing the room with me for what they had to put up with. They did so gracefully. The poor student nurse took away the commode and kindly sprayed air freshener while I went to clean myself up properly. My dignity had been kept intact. What is more important, I was able to have a good sleep.

The staff were fabulous, but not enough to make this an experience I hope to revisit. Once is enough.

I cannot believe I have written so much on the topic, but it shows how important it is for us to have a good 'pooh' regularly. And illness and recovery are not always very pleasant, but it makes a great difference to have people willing to help and who treat one with dignity.

On a different note, I will go back to 12 October. That was another eventful day. I had a slight scare with my right breast. By 8:00 a.m. I was Nil by mouth, not allowed to ingest anything. I had to have an ultrasound to determine if there was a collection of fluid in the right breast. There was no porter to take me there, though, so it had to wait. Finally, around noon, I was wheeled to the ultrasound by an auxiliary nurse who had only returned to work two days prior from recovering from a fractured ankle. It was an interesting ride. I had been asked to go there myself, i.e., to walk with the drains and wearing the hospital's funky designer gown; but I was saved from that, as a wheelchair was found and we successfully manoeuvred our way. The ultrasound was taken and 6x6 collection of fluid was detected.

Not encouraging. The threat of having to go back to theatre for more surgery began to loom over my head.

Steve from the BBC came around 12:10 p.m. to say that they were interested in televising me. Then I had begun to have second thoughts, as my mind had begun to focus on the prospect of a second visit to the theatre.

I thought and then decided I would still do the interview. How could I give up my two or three minutes of fame for a surgery that may and or not happen later in the day? Not only that, I had a story to tell, a message to pass on to others out there who may be undecided on what they wanted to do if they were facing a cancer diagnosis. We all need each other one way or another, and we all have a story to share. This was an opportunity to pass on a message of hope, and if only one person was able to take anything away from my experience, so be it. So I went ahead and it went well.

The TV crew were brilliant. I will be getting a copy of the tape, and I hope I do not cringe when I see myself on TV. It is to be hoped that I won't sound horrible or look as ugly onscreen as I feel. I am not sporting the best hairstyle in the world at present.

Immediately after the interview, the consultants came and confirmed that they would do a local surgical procedure. So they suctioned the fluid at my bed. They removed a number of millilitres of excess fluid. I felt some relief.

Finally, I had something to eat, as I had been NBM for all that tiring day.

My colleagues from work Laura, Pauline and Marion my team came to visit. It was great. They wanted to see my new 'boobs.' When I showed them, they said the Plastic surgeons had done an excellent job.

It felt so good to see the girls. We had a good team. I have had many well-wishers, many cards, and plenty of flowers. I know I told many people. I am sure sharing about my condition is what I needed, and I am glad to so many have remembered me and shared their support.

I realised early that although recovery is a personal journey that one has to embark upon, I needed people to walk behind. This way, when I slowed down or felt like giving up, they were there to gently nudge me on and let me know that there are people who will walk with me.

It has been a humbling experience as well to know how vulnerable I am, and how we can lose total control of our lives so easily. It also reinforces something I already know, which is that no one is indispensable. Life goes on no matter what. That is why we owe it to ourselves to live our lives to the full. To be both dependent and independent of each other.

I am delighted with how I have been aware of my surroundings, able to appreciate gestures of kindness, able to recognise that others also have their crosses to carry. Yes, we all have crosses to carry, and yet total strangers are willing to encourage you to continue. I am grateful that I have been able to challenge and even question my faith and hope without feeling bad about it. I am glad that I have shown, like any other person, that I can be weak as I can be strong. I have always known I have inner strength, and times like this simply reinforce what I already know about the person that I have been and am becoming. I am no shrinking violet.

Some things are important, but some things are more important than others. What I have learned about myself is especially valuable.

14 October

My consultant, Mr Ross, made it very clear that I was not to go home until I was ready to go.

I am now ready to go home. All my drains have come out, and my stitches have been partially removed. For the first time I have put on my own pyjamas in hospital. There is only one word for this and it is progress. Time is a great healer. There are certain things you cannot rush, things that will happen in their own time. My healing is going to happen gradually. I am going to try my best to enjoy the ride and not hurry the process. I am currently not seeking anything, and not terribly anxious about anything. One day at a time, I say.

I had more visitors: Vigey, Ola, Auntie Roli, Mama, Uncle Godfrey, Kwesi, Ese, Charles, Josef, Chudi, Femi, Teju Auntie Anire, Alero. Excellent. Uncle Godfrey brought fruits and supermalt drink. Vigey brought food. People have been ever so nice. I was not left alone at all during my stay in hospital.

My friend Risi, I remember the day you came to visit. Just a couple of weeks before, you had your lovely daughter. You came all the way from Thames Mead with a beautiful bouquet of flowers. You sat by my bed and told a little bit about yourself.

Until then, we had been acquaintances, but from that day on, we have become very good friends, even soul mates.

Sunday, 15 October

I have been in hospital for ten good days now. It is my time to go home, and I am ready to face the outside world and carry on living.

The scariest thing about what has happened is how life goes on. It simply does not stop because you have been in hospital. My bills are waiting for me, along with, more pleasantly, correspondence I have to respond to. Nothing has changed.

Time has gone by so quickly for me and I have not been bored in the slightest.

I was finally discharged today, on 15 October. Thelma, Ayulie, Jnr and Demi came for me. They brought me my clothes. I was leaving the care, comfort, safety and security that the hospital provided. It seemed strange but exciting.

Still, I had some reservations regarding my health. From now on, I would not have the hospital staff around to help if I began to feel pain or have another complication. I am still physically weak, and often tired. I have no clue if the cancer will return or not. Frankly, when I think about it I am petrified at being released into the outside world. I am recovering, but still in immense pain, and I can do very little for myself.

I have no one to look after me apart from my two boys, and they are both in school. Family and friends have their own routines, so one can only expect them to come when they have a window of opportunity. In hospital you are surrounded by human beings always. Even when you fall asleep, you know there are people around.

HOME SWEET HOME

I returned home a week ago today, and since then I have made good progress. Being back has done me a world of good. There is nowhere and nothing like your own home. Wearing my own clothes. Sleeping in my own bed, or lying down on the couch in the living room. It's especially welcome just to have the presence of Ayulie and Junior again. Seeing them every day is such a joy and a relief. My body still hurts from the surgery. Unfortunately this healing process is going to be slow. I am feeling extremely bored, restricted and utterly, utterly frustrated.

To quote Alan Cohen, 'It takes a lot of courage to release the familiar and seemingly secure, to embrace the new. But there is no real security in what is no longer meaningful. There is more security in the adventurous and exciting, for in movement there is life, and in change there is power.'

When I left my home to go to the hospital on 4 October, so many things crossed my mind. I did not know if I would ever return. I certainly did not return the same—during the ten days that I was in hospital, I actually lost my breasts, a part of me. I was familiar with my boobs, but when I got home I was able to have a good look at the reconstruction. It took me quite aback. I had to find the courage to lose the familiar and embrace these new boobs and physique. It changes one. I did not have nipples. Instead, I had scars, and I had to embrace these scars that will be with me all my life. There was no security in holding onto cancerous cells, and that is what my breasts had become. Thus I had to let go of them and receive these new ones.

I had no choice. Or perhaps my choice was to embrace the new, and embark on an adventure with the new, improved me.

Without really being aware of it, I was also changing as a person. Cancer changes one without our realizing it.

What happened once I returned home was alarming. While I was in hospital, I had no time to ponder and look at my body. I was all wired up and in too much pain to even care what I looked like. But on getting out, I had time on my hands to take a good look at my body.

The new boobs make me look like a man in my own eyes. They make my chest broad. I have no nipples! I keep coming back to that fact. These new breasts are smaller and scarred. I have to think really hard about how my boobs looked before the reconstruction—I simply cannot recall.

What I did not do, and should have done, is take before and after pictures. Before letting them go, I should have said farewell to my old boobs and said a silent prayer to wish them well and thank them for serving me all these years.

So here is my Ode to my boobs:

Oh my dear boobs, we have been separated from each other forever more. It hurts to say goodbye, but you understand that if I kept you, I would not have a life for too long. You were lovely and made me feel feminine. Goodbye, and I hope you will remember me as I will remember you as being a part of me. You know that nothing can ever replace you. You were my original, God-given boobs. Nothing now can compare to you. Fare thee well, dear bosom of mine, till we meet again.

Good Lord, look after my boobs for me. They are making their way to you, preparing to be reunited with me whenever you deem fit. They have made the ultimate sacrifice by allowing themselves to be severed from my body so the rest of that body might live a while longer. So please look after them until we are reunited. Thank you, Lord.

***

Monday 23 October

Woke up this morning. I am alive to write in my journal.

I cannot recall what happened on Wednesday and Thursday. On Friday, I went to the hospital for my appointment. I saw the nurse practitioner, who removed my remaining stitches, except for some which have been left inside to dissolve on their own. We talked about my right breast, and I mentioned that I felt fluid accumulating again. The nurse called a doctor, who recommended I go for another ultrasound. I was finally seen around 3:40 p.m. The ultrasound showed that there was indeed an accumulation of fluid. I had 215 ml syringed out, in what was luckily a rather painless procedure.

Afterwards, I went home to get Ayulie ready for his party. As I have mentioned in my journal, nothing stops, life goes on. Ayulie had a party to go to. I was not going to keep him from living his life. As I was not able to start driving again just yet, my Auntie Roli and Uncle Godfrey came to help me drop him off. My brother came round later to help me pick him up.

The right side of my abdomen had been hurting, so that I was wondering if the wound had been infected. Something else to keep an eye on.

Saturday was a very, very busy day. I had many visitors who came to spend time with me. Auntie Fulani, my mother's friend, and her son Charlie came, and so did my mother, Jumai, Muna, and Josef. Josef brought along six lovely bottles of red and white wine. How thoughtful of him. Gaby came briefly to say hi, as he was on route to New York by way of Amsterdam. He brought me some boubous that I had requested. As my tummy and boobs were tender, it was practical for me to wear loose-fitting garments that would not cause any pain or restrict my movements.

24 October

I am beginning to feel irritated and frustrated again, purely because I am anxious about tomorrow's session at the hospital. I made up my mind that I will not be having chemotherapy. All the sovereign's horses and all the ruler's men will not make me have chemo. I will listen to the pros and cons of this chemotherapy thing. Yet I just don't have the energy to be sick. I've had enough to do recovering from the surgery. I don't have the nerve to sit there and allow this toxin to be pumped into my body. The mere thought of it is making my tummy churn.

My thoughts are making me feel trapped and lonely. This whole cancer thing is not working for me. I am fed up with it. I thought (though it was wishful thinking on my part) that surgery would be enough. It would have to be, because chemotherapy is a no-no. The more I read about it, the more I know that I would rather die than have that nasty stuff, that mess of toxins put into my body. Thank goodness for modern technology!

I saw the oncologist and my consultant on Wednesday. Mr Singh, my breast cancer consultant, told me that the good news: out of 17 lymph glands taken during my operation, the cancer had spread to only one. The biopsy confirmed it. Surgery was successful. We were all pleased— now that is what you call a result. I always had faith in surgery because surgery is certain, concrete. Surgeons go in and take out the nasty and close you up, no hassle, no questions asked. It's about precision.

I am terribly pleased about my surgery and beginning to appreciate my new, improved look. The only problem I seem to have is pain in my right breast. It seems as though there is a hard lump beginning to form. I will point this out at my next hospital appointment.

Then came the meeting with oncologist. She actually amused me, as she was not prepared to hear that I wasn't interested in going down the chemotherapy route. She told me outright that if I did not have chemotherapy there is a ten percent chance of the cancer coming back. I was really not fazed by that. I am not scared of chemo; I just don't want it. Fear has never been my guide in life, and I will not start that now.

The conversation was beginning to get boring and academic, as I knew from the moment of diagnosis that I had no intention of having chemotherapy. That was one of the reasons I had such radical surgery. So let's put it this way: the meeting did not go very well. I left with no plans or date to have chemotherapy. I was pleased with myself for maintaining control of my treatment. Believe it or not, none of my replies were rehearsed. I was not trying to be clever. I simply said that I would not be having chemotherapy. Not now, not ever, non-negotiable. Words just came to me. My spirit must have been guiding me through the process. I have never experienced chemotherapy, but something within me knows that it is not really what I need right now.

Thanks to my surgery, I think I am in a better position to gradually process and understand what cancer is about. The surgery has allowed me to heal, to think and to process. Before it even happened, I had already told Mr Singh my thoughts on chemotherapy and radiotherapy. He did tell me he would let me off on radiotherapy, but he also stressed he would not let me go without chemotherapy. Well, that was his opinion.

It is inconceivable that I should have subjected myself to thirteen hours of surgery for no reason. And if it was not a one-stop shop for me, then what was the reason?

So, first off, now that chemotherapy comes up I feel certain in my mind that it is not necessary.

As I met with the oncologist, I knew I was the owner of my body. I had reached a point where I took ownership of my cancer. I never asked for cancer, but I strongly believe it is my right to accept ownership of it and to deal with it. And having taken ownership meant the battle was already won, irrespective of the outcome. I was not a victim of cancer. I was only diagnosed with it. And I am the only constant in my cancer journey—every other person, including physicians, were variables. So it was a very simple exercise to say 'no' to them when they offered something I didn't want. Just like turning down any offer when I don't want to buy what you are selling.

And silence is not an option when your life is on the line.

My motto has always been, and always will be, 'let not fear be your guide, but God.' Or the 'Supreme Being' if you prefer.

Of course, in your own mind you can agree to disagree with your consultants, oncologists, or whoever. But believe it or not—and I believe it—whether you agree or disagree, it is always by some divine intervention. Listen to your heart and hear what it says. It is that invisible force, guiding you in one direction or the other, whichever is best to get to the desired outcome destined for your life.

At the end of the day, only God knows when and how one will depart from the beautiful world He created. We believe we have the power to do things, but what we do is merely an intervention. That is all that it is. And yet once I have made up my mind, I will stick to it and accept the consequences.

Another day and another hospital appointment. The appointments are many, haba! Too many. It is difficult for me because I hurt all over. Walking is not easy; I am all bent over trying to ease the pain. Back at St Thomas', my appointment got all mixed up. My name was cancelled for some reason. Oh, never mind, what do I care? Eventually I got to be seen by the doctor, who confirmed that there was another build-up of fluid on the right side of my breast. The doctor says I should leave it for the time being so that it can drain itself. Now it has turned to a hard lump. We will see. Movement of my right hand is still restricted.

Today I received a lovely card from an individual who saw me on City Hospital, the BBC1 programme I took part in while in hospital. I did say if I could reach out to at least one person then going on television would have been worth it. My Auntie Roli was in the hospital with me when the programme was recorded. She stood in the wings, just watching and listening to what I said. She told me that she had told some of her friends that her niece was going to be on TV. But for my own part, I do not recall telling anyone else about the programme, as it had been unplanned—just something to do while I was in hospital. At the time, I was feeling emotionally numb. But my words have touched a stranger enough to make them write to me. I reached the one person. I thank God for that. A tiny drop makes a mighty ocean.

I have still not found the passion to pick up my books and study. I still have the strength to write, because I have been writing in journals all my life and I am not about to stop now. Writing at a time like this seems natural.

Lest I forget, I saw a counsellor. It was a good session. All I have to do is talk, all she had to do was listen. She however, did ask me some pertinent questions. Maybe I was expecting too much of myself? Maybe I need to try to be a little bit more gentle and kinder to myself?

I went for my first long walk on Saturday. I still don't know how I did it, but I must have been gone for three hours, just walking, taking in and appreciating nature. My tummy hurt, my boobs hurt, but I could not help myself or stop myself from walking and walking and walking. It was good because it took my mind off things.

31 October

It has been four weeks since I had my surgery. I am making good progress. I am able to move about lots more and do so much more for myself, which is a relief. All of a sudden I had thought I was losing myself. It is not the best to have to depend on others to do everything for you. I have been quite fortunate that my boys have been so good. They have not complained. For teenagers, they have behaved like absolute angels.

I went for another walk through Crystal Palace Park on Sunday. Most delightfully, I was not puffed out—exercise did not make me breathless.

I think I am beginning to feel bored as I am now regaining my strength. There are a number of things I cannot do yet. The numbness in my right hand is gradually going, but I still have my limitations. I cannot stretch the right hand too far or it will hurt. My tummy is beginning to take shape, but there is still a bit of swelling the left side.

I bought a rug yesterday, a bright coloured one. I need some sunshine in my life. I need that ray of happiness to flicker past me whenever I go through that room. I need to raise my spirits. I am hoping the walks in the park will do the trick, but it is still early days.

I took out my hair attachments. I did not fancy the style anyway. I will go back to my usual single braided plaits, something that I feel comfortable with.

I am looking forward to driving again for the first time since surgery. It is to be hoped that it will not be too much of an ordeal. I wish I had a magic wand to wish away all the bills and transport me to a beautiful place for a holiday. It is not like I cannot go on a holiday, but it would require sacrifices, alternatives forgone. Something or someone would have to give or suffer.

My other worry is work. I have only two months full pay and five months half-pay. Unfortunately, I cannot survive on half pay. If I could I would simply take the whole seven months off, get on with this so-called chemotherapy, complete my studies and return to work in July. I have had several calls from the breast cancer nurses, urging me to reconsider my decision not to have chemotherapy. My auntie and friends have also quietly had a word here and there, asking me to reconsider. But it would take so much out of me, and I need to have money to live while I take these toxins, getting sick to get better.

I have to work this out and check again what benefits I may be entitled to, if any. What a palaver.

When the body is not sound, it is highly unlikely that the mind and soul will be sound. It is one thing to have to navigate complicated things like benefits. Meanwhile, I am also trying really hard to see if my creative mind will open up. Time will tell. One day I will wake up and experience that light bulb moment.

1 November

Got my hair plaited yesterday. I am beginning to look like myself again.

I did dream of returning to college and getting all my notes sorted. I am sure I will do it by the weekend if I want to catch up, but I'm beginning to lack the passion and drive to continue.

3 November

I woke up this morning thinking to myself that no poor person has any business having cancer. It is so easy for people to say 'have this treatment, have that treatment.' Treatment that keeps you off work, reduces your income. And no single person has any business having cancer. What a heavy cross to carry. It is an emotional, physical and mental burden when you are on your own with limited resources.

Who should I turn to so that I can express my concerns, my worries? Support groups are all well and good but people are far removed. I don't feel like anyone there would really understand what I am going through. People can empathise; I guess the good thing about support groups is they are able to point you in the right direction with the help you need, financial or emotional.

It is not right that anyone should have cancer of any sort. It is right that people who have cancer can choose their treatment, and decline any treatment they feel is not right for them. Life goes on, people keep going. My pet hate about this cancer issue is having to rely on people and not being in a stronger financial position. I cannot sleep again because I am worrying and stressing myself out again. I don't know why I bother, but unfortunately I do. I try so much to remain calm and just go with the flow, but I am finding it so difficult. Everything is so busy and stressful. When it comes to human beings, I belong to the school of thought that we were not brought to earth to be mother, father, cleaner, cook, driver, bread provider, student worker, etc. all rolled into one. It is so not right. The developed countries may have many advantages, but one of the greatest disadvantages is the whole DIY culture. It may be one of the reasons why people are burning out so fast, getting stressed out and depressed.

I digress. I had a good day yesterday. On Thursday I went into Croydon, Whitgift Shopping centre on my own—that is, I drove there. Yes! It was a remarkable experience. I spent a lot of time in Marks & Spencer trying to find the right lingerie for my new and improved body. I got myself measured and selected a proper bra to suit post-surgery. Marks & Spencer have so many pretty things in their store, especially in the lingerie and nightwear sections. Very dainty.

They were celebrating their 100th birthday, so there was plenty of free flowing champagne, orange juice and wine. I spent a couple of hours just looking, as I was bone idle. But it did take my mind off things. Along with my bra, I ended up buying a couple of microfiber tee-shirts. I have to be careful what fabrics I allow against my skin, as it is now very sensitive. I also went into Wallis and bought a couple of nice tops. Pleased with my purchases, I then drove home again.

Then I took my son Ayulie to the GP. He has got a chest infection and was prescribed some antibiotics.

I am thoroughly enjoying going on my long walks, and I aim to go for a walk every day. It is getting a bit cold, though, and I have not yet found a good coat to wear.

When one gets cancer, one does not have a template or prescribed form describing the highs and lows to come. Seriously, moods begin to take on a life of their own. Nothing can prepare you for it. They do not provide you with any warning; they decide what mood you will be in whether you like it or not. The moods play jokes on you. I believe I need to write my Ode to Moods, because one of the moods has taken over:

Oh Mood! Oh Mood! Which mood am I dealing with now? Is it my good mood or my bad mood, my sad mood or happy mood or my nonchalant mood? Oh mood—

Why do you not give me any warning when you come to me? Why do you choose the mood you will be? You make me believe I have a choice about how I will feel, but Mood, that is not the case. You switch when you decide. You inhabit my mind and play games with all the other moods. It is like playing roulette with you, Mood. You moody trickster. How do you choose your mode, Mood? Why are you as unpredictable as the weather? I guess if you were not that way, you would not be known as moody. Mood, you are temperamental, and you take us on roller coaster rides: such highs and such lows.

But without you, Mood, we would not be able to appreciate when we are happy or sad, good or bad.

5 November

Exactly a month to the date I had my surgery. The 5th of October seems such a long time ago. I am getting stronger with each passing day. What is done is done, I suppose. It is what it is. I am trying not to dwell on my situation.

I could say I am still in a state of denial. I feel as though I am a performer that had a role to play. I have completed my role and am back to my normal self.

I now have to prepare for the next role, as that is the role of chemotherapy. I still have not got my head around it.

I have been receiving more telephone calls from the breast cancer nurse at Princess Royal, asking me to reconsider my stance about chemotherapy. I really wish I could be left alone. I have been told I only have a three-month window of opportunity, and if I do not start chemo before January it will be pointless.

I have also been talked to by family and friends. They tell me that even if I don't want to take chemotherapy for myself, I should think about my son and take chemotherapy so that he will have a mother around for a bit longer. To me, that was just some form of emotional blackmail. If you read about what this chemotherapy is, and heard the experiences of people who have done it, you will agree with me it is a no-no.

In the meantime, I have other plans for my life which do not involve chemotherapy. Why are they all messing with my already fragile head? Urrgh. Leave me alone, please!

It's not like I can't take chemotherapy if push comes to shove, but I want to take it much later, say September next year. I don't know why that cannot be possible. I want to complete my LPC. Whether I pass or fail the assessments is no longer here or there. I just want to put a closure to it.

I am also trying to figure out what I want to do on returning to work. The mere thought of going back to deal with clients' complaints simply does not appeal to me at all right now. I only have to read about work and I know I have no desire to return. But I have to work to bring home the bacon to put on the table, or however the phrase goes.

I am not a quitter, but things are getting pretty rough right now.

I understand that when you begin to sow you come across so many obstacles. The soil may not be fertile, with too much rain making it soggy, too much sun making it hard; but there will come a time when the soil is just right and things begin to grow beautifully. Then there will be the time to reap what you have sown. Life is like that. The time to reap will happen, as no condition is permanent. It rained for forty days and forty nights but then it stopped raining. That is the way the good Lord made the earth we live in.

6 November

On Monday, I went to see the plastic surgeons. I had a very long wait in the outpatient clinic. Once I got in to see them, they were pleased with my progress and said I should see them again in another three months. Yippee.

The chemotherapy issue has raised its ugly head again. I have been asked to give it some thought. I have been giving chemo a thought. I am yet to be convinced why I should have it. I am feeling very well in myself and beginning to see things a bit clearer now.

7 November

I stayed home today, no walking or shopping. I am feeling a wee bit tired. I managed to read John Diamond's book on cancer, *C: Because Cowards Get Cancer Too*.... It was magnificent, brilliant read. I could identify with many of his feelings, his distaste for the numerous cancer clichés of being brave and 'staying positive.' It is difficult to be brave when one did not chose cancer, but instead cancer chose you. More often than not, we just deal with it. I identify most especially with his reaction to the news he had cancer. In my experience, it is not earth shattering news, although we all react differently. I guess having been both mother and father, and being on my own for the past 14 years, I am hardened so that not many things can move me, including my own cancer diagnosis. In a way I have been equipped to deal with stressful situations. People will say I am strong—that is rubbish. As human beings we all have the capacity to be weak or strong. It is a choice. All you have to do is look around you and identify your safety net. If you don't have that safety net, how on earth can you indulge in what we call being weak?

We all know how to survive, and weakness is not part of it. When the chips are down our survival mechanism steps in. If you have loads of support and a good, secure safety net financially and emotionally, of course you have the permission to be weak! Be my guest and be weak. I would love to be able to be weak.

It is so easy for people in a relationship to say, Oh! But it might not be any better if you were in a relationship. Hmm, I do wish they would kindly keep quiet. There is a difference between being on you own and being a part of union, group, team, whatever you wish to call it. There is strength in numbers.

John Diamond was so honest. At least, he did think at some point, his suffering must end. Despite treatment, his cancer killed him aged 47.

Why should people suffer so much? Even animals are put down to stop their suffering, so why should humans continue to endure hardship, poverty, disease, unhappiness? Yeh! Yeh! I can hear someone say: what about happiness, pleasure, contentment, stability? Humans have these even more than animals. Yes, I know these, but they seem so elusive. For the majority they are hard to come by. That's the way the world is.

Life sometimes comes across as more a con than a pro, and Earth seems a highly overrated planet to be living on.

10 November

My boss from work came to see me. It was a whistle stop visit, but it was very kind of him. He also mentioned that I should consider taking chemotherapy, as 'it does what it says on the tin.' Hmm.

I went to my son's school to see his maths teacher to discuss his targets and academic review. Mummy duties cannot be put on hold. You have to do what you have to do to keep the wheel turning. I am happy I can still carry out my duties, no matter what. My son needs me.

I was able to view my college work properly for the first time and will be returning on Monday. I have missed almost two weeks of lectures and tutorials. Not the best for a professional course, where attendance is highly important. There is plenty to catch up on, and I will have to give it my best shot. What do I have to lose? Not a lot. Hard work has never been known to kill anyone. Boredom and idleness, on the other hand, have.

I read some beautiful poetry about cancer on the internet. It was awesome. Plenty of inspirational and realistic stuff on it. I have healed from surgery and am healing mentally. I have to get back into my routine, once more being busy and doing things.

11 November

Last night I slept well, but had horrible dream about chemo. I know I ought to get on with it, but it is awful. Let us call a spade a spade. Knowing what the side effects are like is not helping me one iota. Why on earth should I want to subject myself to this? It is hard, I must admit. I am not scared, because I know I will get through it if I must. I just don't want all the toxins in my body.

12 November

A thought for today: Live your life and use your life so that the use of your life outlives your life.

The weather is wonderful. With the autumn leaves and sunshine, today is truly a beautiful Sunday. I am getting stronger, my mind is becoming clearer and I am beginning to become more focused. Nothing lasts forever, not even sadness. Along with happiness, it has its place in our lives.

Speaking of sadness, though, I don't understand why I have not been able to cry. I guess I need my strength, and tears right now may be a waste. Yet they could possibly help me come to terms with how my life has been out of my control so extremely lately. Little things, like a cuddle now and again, are missing; somebody just telling me that they care is missing, just a simple gesture like helping me go to the shops and manage my shopping is missing. My boys are doing a great job. Maybe it is just me. I know I have friends and family who will help me if I pick up the phone, but I seem to be devoid of emotion and unable to reach out to anyone.

I talk about events, talk about the problems I am meeting with or will come across, and that's it.

I am praying that things will work out for the best. It is human to go through periods of darkness and then periods of light. As I was saying, sadness and happiness each have their place and each will pass. That is the reason we have the four seasons. Every season we see things differently. The same thing, the same view, the same tree, will not look the same in summer as in autumn.

Looking at it this way makes me feel more inspired. Life is for the living, so if you want to live life you have to go for it. Do things differently, take calculated and uncalculated risks. Some things will work for you and some things won't work. That is the beauty of it all. As it has been said, what man proposes, God disposes. We can never know ahead of time how things will turn out. We only know that in time, they will change again, with the coming of another season.

13 November

I went to college today, and it was one of the best days I have had in a long time. I sorted out my college stuff: property law, interviewing. I still must sort out my civil litigation. I will get there eventually, working persistently. I must try not to put myself under any undue pressure. The last thing I want to do is break down because I am trying to catch up. The way I look at it, I cannot lose in this situation. If I succeed, it will be an added bonus; if I don't make it, it won't be for lack of trying. That is all I can do.

I am feeling happier and re-energised. I am also feeling stronger, and I think psychologically I am ready for chemo. I do not know how I will react to the next stage of treatment, but I know I will get through it.

15 November

When is it going to be right time for me to start chemo? I wonder. I really don't have too many options other than gritting my teeth and getting on with it. The sooner I start, the sooner I will get it over with and get over it.

Funny, right now I am back to my optimistic, enthusiastic self. Obviously this is not going to last. The minute stage two of treatment kicks in the darkness will probably fall again. I had better start thinking on how to reinvent myself. God, give me the strength to get through chemo, the same way you gave me the strength to get through surgery. It is really hard to motivate oneself all the time.

16 November

I went to the office to discuss my sick pay. While I was there, I seized the opportunity to see colleagues and friends. The meeting went very well. It was agreed I will be on full pay for three months. Past that, there is not much I can do; I will have to take one day at a time. It is a start, and much better than nothing.

I have decided I will embark on the chemo. Frankly, I am getting tired of well-wishers urging me to just give it a go. Easy for them to say!

After the office, I went to college. Class was tiring. Yet afterwards I walked along Oxford Street, taking in all the lights.

17 November

Can't get over myself. I made the dreaded telephone call to Jane, the breast care nurse, to let her know that I was ready to have chemo. She was absolutely delighted that I was going to give myself a chance. One would have thought I had won the lottery. She immediately arranged a pre-assessment, which is to take place 22 November.

I am not looking forward to it, but I am mentally and emotionally prepared to take the next step. I guess I have to see chemo as cure and not a punishment, however physically difficult it may be. I know I will get by no matter what. My life is in the hands of the Almighty God above, and it is to Him I look up.

23 November

'No two women will respond exactly the same way to chemotherapy,' I've read over the course of my research. 'Get through the first treatment, and then plan your life around what happens to you.' So I will be taking it one day a time, as always.

Today I went to the treatment suite at Princess Royal to have a work out (that is what pre-chemo assessment is called). When I walked into the treatment suite, I burst into tears. It was overwhelming. I could not believe how emotional I was. At a guess, this was because I knew deep down that I do not want chemo. It has only opened fresh wounds. It brought home that I am not yet 100% cured.

At least I enjoyed the walk from the station to the hospital and back to the station. I was in tip top shape. The weather was wonderful, fresh and crisp. What is more important, it was good exercise. I will try to keep it up despite chemo, even if it means just walking in the park.

24 November

My son Ayulie's 14th birthday. How time flies. Fourteen long years of love, joy, sorrow, illness and laughter. All the pain long forgotten. We all went to watch Casino Royale, starring Daniel Craig as James Bond. I thought that was a movie well worth watching, and we had an excellent time. Ayulie got many ££££'s for his birthday. Good for him.

It was a good day.

27 November

Today I did some Christmas shopping. Along the way, I went to the office to drop off Christmas cards and presents for the team. I stopped to see Jumai; she bought me a drinks flask. Extremely thoughtful of her.

Tuesday, 28 November

The dreaded chemo day has finally arrived. Auntie Roli and Uncle Godfrey came to pick me up from home and take me to the hospital.

After being checked to ensure that my white blood count was okay, I was taken to the suite where there were many other patients having chemo.

I was told that the best-looking patients in the room were the patients with breast cancer, as their physical appearance did not change over the course of treatment. Some of the other patients had gone darker or ashen in colour.

I was given a chair to sit in and the chemo was inserted into my vein as a drip. It was a bit of a task as the nurse had difficulty locating a vein. Then the process started. The chemo thingy is actually covered up with grey plastic so you don't see it. All cloak and dagger to me. My thoughts really went all over the place. Why were we not allowed to see the actual drug? Why was it all covered up? Spooky, ha ha.

Some anti-sickness solution was administered, then finally the dreaded chemo itself. Delivered intravenously. Saline—antibiotics—E (red)—F—C. Saline. Together the chemo combination I had is called FEC. The drip itself took approximately one hour, and it was not too bad. You sit there watching it go through your veins. I was offered a cold cap to protect my hair from falling out. Really? A nurse had already told me that the cold cap would not really stop my hair from falling out, owing to the texture of my African hair. But the cold cap was actually cold. I don't think I will be using it again

Once we got home, my Auntie wanted to stay with me, but I thought she had done enough for one day. I felt okay, at least for the next two hours. After that I started having a blinding headache and feeling nauseous.

My boys came back from school and Dukuye decided to sleep over to make sure I was okay. I slept for the whole day and cannot remember having anything to eat.

I had the first chemo session on Tuesday. Wednesday, Thursday and Friday were the worst days of my waking life regarding this all-singing, all-dancing chemo.

I was sick, lost my appetite, even brought up bile. I felt really rough and awful. The only way I can describe the experience like having morning sickness, but ten times worse.

My emotions were on a roller coaster. I have questioned my sanity: was it a wise decision to embark on chemo? I will never know for certain. I felt so alone. Mama, Ayulie, Demi, Jnr, Thelma, Auntie Roli, Uncle Godfrey and Dukuye were all supportive, but none of it helped. Bimbo and Amaka from West Africa called to check that I was okay. It was nice to know that my old school mates and friends still care about my wellbeing. For all that, it is a long, lonely road, this cancer malarkey. I cannot wait for it to end.

Still, I cannot complain about my well-wishers or the support I have received from family and friends.

6 December

OMG, it has been a week since I had my first chemo session. I woke up and my tongue was black and blue. I am reacting to chemo in a bad way. How scary!

10 December

Chemo, chemo, chemo. Whoever came up with such a concoction? My hair is finally falling out. I took one of my braids down and it fell straight off from my scalp. Smack bang in the face, hair loss, just as I was beginning to feel good again—it's so unfair. One can never be prepared for it. We all know it is going to happen, but no amount of preparation can help you handle such difficult situations. I will have to get my hair shaved off this week.

I have a wig fitting session at Princess Royal on Friday. Another change for me. How does one embrace change of such a nature and remain positive? I do not have the answers. It is really hard. It may seem easy to say, it is just hair, it will grow back! I know that, but I did not choose to have cancer. Even though something like this is easily fixed with time, I never asked for it. No wonder I am beginning to lose my faith.

12 December

I did not want to lose my hair, but it comes with the territory. I went alone to a barber and told them shave everything off. As my braids fell to the ground, so did my tears. I have had to bury another part that has been with me for a long time.

My hair. Bye bye.

My good friend Daniel had already told me he would shave his hair off if it made me feel better. The words were like music to my ears, and it was sweet to think that my friend would actually do that to support me. He came over with Katy and bought me some headwear as a gift from both of them and his daughter. Bless.

I had been under no illusions that chemo would be a walk in the park, but it is not pleasant at all. I guess so long as you are alive and hopeful, you will be able to get through it.

During chemo, and while my hair was being shaved, I felt sad, but not as bad as I thought I would. I presume my subconscious had been preparing for the day to come. What I was not prepared for was the reaction waiting at home.

Surgery does not change one's physical appearance, especially not with the plastic surgeons doing their reconstruction. However, chemo does. By this stage, even though it was my first session of chemo, I had started losing weight. I had not been able to eat, had been sick a lot and was just feeling horrible.

On the day I went to have my hair shaved off, the boys had gone to school. An image that will be etched in my memory for all eternity was my son's reaction when he came home.

When he returned from school, my head was bald—cancer staring us in the face. Ayulie could not look at me. He had his head down. The reality that I had cancer was now glaring, out in the open. Mummy is not well, she is truly sick. I had nowhere to hide.

The back of my head was so cold. I had to tie a scarf on immediately. From that point onwards, I have always made a conscious or unconscious effort to keep my head covered.

17 December

My first chemo has been traumatic and horrible. But how can I forget to say that my son Jnr has just been a star? When I was sick, Ayulie would say, 'Jnr, Jnr, Mum is being sick.' Jnr would quietly come in the bathroom and rub my back. He is only 15 years old.

Ayulie and Jnr go to Sainsbury's to do the grocery shopping when I cannot physically get out of bed. They have learnt how to cook jollof rice and fend for themselves. My heart is in bits just seeing them look after themselves. They just get on with it.

And how can I forget Thelma? She comes after work every day to make me something to eat. All I want is pepper soup and starch, an Itsekiri dish. It is simple, easy to make and easy to eat. Good for my palate. She makes it for me before going home to sort herself and her daughter out. What a juggling act.

I will never forget lying down in my bedroom with the windows wide open and feeling boiling hot. My room was like a freezer, but I did not feel the cold. How can I explain that chemo is like someone taking a gun to my head? My brains blowing out and my head exploding? I hold my head and rock it, wishing I could die. How can I describe how little I can tolerate smells? Parfum is a killer; I cannot let anyone wearing parfum come near me because it makes me so sick. There are no words to describe the impact of chemo on me. I knew it and I said it, chemo and I are not compatible.

Oh, but health professionals think they know it all. No, they don't. They can assist, but they should not impose. We need to listen more to our inner voice. It is there for a reason, and the reason is to guide us. We should not ignore it.

Chemo has made me lose my faith. I have had to question how God, my father in heaven, could allow me to go through such pain. I thought God was a loving God, a kind God, a merciful God. There's nothing kind or merciful about chemo.

I have asked my friends who have faith and who believe to use their faith to see me through chemo, as I have no faith left in me to praise the Lord. So my friends, you need to be strong for me.

Psalm 121 says, 'I lift up my mine eyes to unto the hills, from whence cometh my help. My help cometh from the Lord, which made Heaven and Earth. He will not suffer thy foot to be moved: he that keepth thee will not slumber.'

At this point it is hard to believe.

18 December

I went to Princess Royal for an aromatherapy session. It's supposed to relax you. The room was right next to the room where chemo is administered. I met Dee the aromatherapist. It was a good and enlightening experience. The room was right next to the outpatient chemotherapy room, but once I stepped in I simply forgot I was in a hospital. The room was small and clean, with a rustic feel to it. The furniture and colour scheme was mahogany and teak. It was dimly lit with candles. In the middle of the room was a bed with white sheets. The smell of aromatherapy oils filled the place. At first all I was aware of was the tranquillity and peacefulness of the room. I felt transported to another place.

Dee was great, and I enjoyed listening to and speaking with her. It turns out she had also had a life-threatening ailment and was able to talk the talk as she had walked the walk. That experience, she explained, was how she got into aromatherapy. It changed her life. Experience is the best teacher. She was able to appreciate my hopes, fears and desires.

I mentioned I was going for a wig fitting session at Princess Royal. It was a real fiasco. I could not believe provision had not been made to supply the right wigs for ethnic minorities, wigs they would prefer to be seen in. I was led into the room where the hair dresser asked me to sit down. She then brought out an array of wigs: blond wigs, black wigs, brunette wigs, I don't know. I have never worn a wig in my life, so presenting me with those wigs was not up my street.

I became visibly upset, and did not take or try on any of the wigs.

I did, however, make my experience known to the breast cancer nurse on my next visit. I offered the suggestion that it might help if the ethnicity of the patient was made known to the hair dresser before the sitting session. That way the hair dresser would be able to possibly bring more suitable wigs. The other thing I could not comprehend there was the lack of alternative forms of headwear. It might have been helpful to have hats, scarves, or something other than wigs to choose from. If the truth be said, it is an extremely sensitive time for cancer patients who have lost their hair. They are likely to become more frustrated than the average person who just wants a wig to be fashionable. My heart goes out to people who have lost their hair and need to rely on wigs. In my case, my hair will at least grow back one day soon.

I am writing in the waiting room at the hospital, being prepared for the second chemo session. My oncologist told me that I am going to have six sessions of chemo in all. So she says. Really, that is her take on it, not mine.

It is not entertaining to have to sit and watch the toxins being pumped into one's body. The very thought of it is making my tummy churn as I write this. I hope my sick feeling is not in my head. I truly hate this regimen, but what on earth can I do about it?

One thing, though: the hospital staff are awfully nice. They treat you with a great deal of sensitivity. It would be nice, though, if they were able to locate my veins sooner rather than later. All this poking about does not help matters.

I will see how this second session pans out. I am not happy to be sick or tired, and will try yet again to avoid both. I just cannot succumb to the side effects.

I just had my blood count checked. My blood count was 1.1, which means I just made it. The cut-off point is 1.0. Thank goodness, I will not be delayed; the chemo will be administered today.

Auntie Roli and Uncle Godfrey took me again, and I left them in the hospital while I go for a walk. I walked to Orpington station from the hospital. It is approximately two miles one way. And then I also walked back! My Auntie and Uncle thought I had done a runner, as if I had chickened out of having the chemo.

But I had time to go for the four mile walk, because the chemo mixture is only prepared when you have been given the all clear that your blood count is okay. It takes a couple of hours for that to be done, so a walk then seemed suitable. I for one was not in any hurry.

I got back to the hospital and obediently went through the motion of watching the toxins being administered into my system. I have already begun to have a headache. I don't care if this is meant to be a permanent cure, it is nasty hindrance to my wellbeing. I hate it. End of!

December 23

It has been almost a week since the second chemo. Monday, Tuesday and Wednesday were ghastly. I spent those days being sick and feeling totally wretched. Chemo has not been kind to me. I hate it with every fibre in my body, and the feeling is mutual.

I wish this nasty nausea feeling would just go away. I have stopped taking the anti-sickness drugs. They are actually making me feel worse. Thursday was a bit more tolerable now that I have stopped taking the tablets. My hands and fingernails have started to become discoloured. My hands look appalling. What can I do? I wish it would go away, but they will be like that for a couple of months.

It is good that I was feeling somewhat better on Thursday, because I was able to take the boys to Croydon to do their Christmas shopping. Bless them. For two teenagers, they are doing okay. I have to keep things as normal as I possibly can. I completed my Christmas shopping and had the presents wrapped up by Lisa Baxter volunteers who set up a stall every Christmas to raise funds for a cancer charity. Now that I am a cancer survivor, it is imperative I put back into society all the money that is being spent on me. I am one of the lucky ones. I can write in this journal when I feel sad or happy, when I have mood swings that go high or low—whatever emotion I feel, I can at least express it. Not everyone is that fortunate.

Despite feeling poorly, I went for a very long walk on Wednesday. I find the walks invigorating. They have helped me so much. Generally I have kept up with them, although how I do it I'm not sure. What I do know is I take one step at a time, one step, then the next and the next.

I have finally decided I am going to see my GP and ask him how I go about getting a second opinion concerning the chemo malarkey. I feel, I know in my hearts of hearts, that my cancer—and I take ownership of my ailment—has gone and gone forever. My spirit feels the same way. I do not need to have any more treatment, chemo and/or anything else, for that matter. It is doing my head in and making me feel awful. Enough is enough. It is time for me to stop and let my own body do the healing. I want to spend the next couple of months getting better and enjoying the days before I return to work.

30 December
The year is surely ending. It has been an interesting year, to say the least.

Christmas Day was peaceful. Auntie Roli invited us to her home for Christmas Day, but I could not go because I could not tolerate the food smells. Thank you, chemo. Killjoy therapy.

So my Ayulie and Junior went with Thelma and Demi to Auntie Roli's. Life goes on, and the boys still have to have fun and do all the things that need to be done. Dukuye stayed home with me. I have been rather content and at peace this week. I am still trying hard to come to terms with the side effects of chemo. Chemo does not get easier; it actually gets progressively worse with each session. The only difference is that one is able to manage it better because one knows what to expect to a certain extent. I must say I had the same or similar reactions the second time around as with the first session. It helped with managing the nausea and throwing up. Yet it is still unpleasant.

More than ever before, I realise and also appreciate that cancer, or any chronic ailment, is a personal journey in your life. There is very little that people can say or do to make the physical, mental and emotional turmoil go away. It is a Catch-22 for everyone involved. What do you say to someone going through chemo? We all look good on the outside, but are going through hell, even dying inside.

I love the way the two other individuals in the treatment suite with me the other day said, the one thing that gets on their nerves is the fact that people keep saying how well they look. It is truly not very clever to say to someone with cancer, 'How well you look!' How should they look? Like death warmed up. It likewise baffles me when you muster up the courage and enthusiasm to speak to people on the phone and they say how well you sound. How should we sound? What use is it to the person listening and to the sufferer to start sounding like the walking dead? All very sad. The listener, more often than not, is not about to drop what they are doing to come and hold your hand and look after you no matter how awful you sounded. Why all this focus on sounding or looking good? At the end of the day, honestly, it is up to the sufferer to determine how they want to live with cancer and the subsequent treatment that follows.

On my part, I have decided to let sunshine in my heart and in my life, and just stay still during the first couple of days of chemo. It is much more stressful to have the pressure off me at those times. Chemo gives me enough to occupy me.

I have gone to the shops, taken part in the sales, enjoyed and embraced the festive season. The chemo was planned and timed that way, and I honestly achieved my objective to be in good health on Christmas Day and New Year's Day. I have been pacing myself well. I've made conscious effort not to think outside my box, that is, of the future. I have lived in the present, which is so unlike me. I am a worrier. I worry a lot, but now I am learning to take each day as it comes and embrace what the day has to offer.

Nothing has really changed physically: my health and other personal problems have not magically disappeared. All that has happened is that I am managing my problems better. I am not stressing about college. I have come to terms that I may never qualify as a solicitor and practice, but I ask myself, does it really matter? It will not take away my self-worth and confidence.

I went to the GP on Friday to discuss my concerns regarding the chemo. I really don't want to continue with the treatment because I can feel within myself that enough is enough. I feel so well, and intuitively I feel the chemo is just an unnecessary topping on the cake, something that I could do without. My GP told me that the final decision is and will be mine. He wrote a letter to the hospital suggesting I have an injection that might help with the nausea. I don't think I will be taking that. Now that I know what to expect, I really don't want to rock the boat with more substances in my body if I do continue with the treatment.

My head tells me that it is a temporary inconvenience, but my heart and body tell me that they lack the strength to carry on. It is difficult when you have to lie there all on your own with only your own thoughts for company. Chemo messes with you head in a way that surgery does not. I would go under the knife any day, any time, rather than go through one more session of chemo. I honestly don't know where I am going to get the strength to go through four more sessions. I was hoping I could leave the health situation behind me in the past, but it seems to me that cancer is going to be with me for the first quarter of the new year. Not a prospect I am looking forward to. Then I should try to fast forward a little bit—once it is over, it shall never be revisited, all things being equal.

When one puts things into perspective, one appreciates when one is in the enviable position to receive good health care. For these problems, there are solutions available. That does not remove the fact that one is human, and it is normal to go through phases of self-pity, sadness, joy, happiness, despondency, hope and laughter.

We all know there are people who are better and worse off in any situation, but that should not be a good enough reason to refrain from your emotions. Just because others are worse off, that does not mean one is not also in an unfortunate situation, worthy of pity from oneself or others.

I have been amazed at friends who have categorically state they do not indulge in self-pity. But my darling friends, you are not the one going through cancer and treatment. The way we handle our situations differs from person to person. Let's be honest, even with the best of intentions, insensitivity, lack of understanding and sheer ignorance is not on. If you don't know what to say, silence is actually good option. Say nothing! By saying nothing, you do not upset the sufferer, who is thinking of his or her own survival technique. Each and every one of us has the innate ability to survive no matter what, but survival is not an exact science. For me, one of my strategies has been to convince myself that every chemo session is my last and I will not be returning the treatment suite. That thought has helped me endure these sessions and enjoy a good two weeks.

I am not strong, I am not a fighter, I am as weak as the next person, but I am a level-headed, logical and analytical survivor! No more, no less. I have been scared, but my motto has been 'Fear is not my guide, let God be my guide.' I have never lived in fear of having cancer and the treatments to cure it. I have been irritated and frustrated with the discomfort my body has to go through, and I have felt lonely during the long days and nights I have to spend on my own. The lack of zeal and energy I have to put towards my legal practice course, these are the things that have made me feel despondent. Having dreams shattered is enough to make anyone feel despondent.

Later

Yeah, I have just come off the internet, and lo and behold: I read the FEC chemo treatment is between 4–6 sessions. Six is the high end—but four! That's it. Bingo, I have hit the jack pot. Hahaha. Gotcha, chemo! Thank goodness for the internet.

1 January—New Year's Day 2007

Entered the New Year peacefully and purposely. Nothing particularly eventful happened. It is just good to be alive and to have Ayulie, Jnr Demi and the rest of the family around. Sometimes it's the simple things that count. No fuss, no frills, just quiet.

January 12

I am waiting to see the oncologist at the Princess Royal to discuss the way forward about the remaining chemo sessions I have left. I have exhausted my vocabulary and adjectives and expressions trying to explain how distasteful chemo is. Anyone reading this journal would have got the message loud and clear by now. Forgive me, allow me to indulge a little more in my frustration and reject the all-singing and toxic chemotherapy. I am not bothered if other people have had chemo and have been able to tolerate it, but theirs has not been my experience. Many people would not bother to have the surgery I did. Each to their own, I say.

One good piece of news: my employers have been very understanding and have used their discretion to continue to pay me in full for another three months. Hallelujah! There is a God. I can only get better quicker if my money worries do not become a major issue.

Thank you sooo much, employers. Nice one!

I sat my solicitors account assessments and handed in my PLR2 assessment. I really put everything I could into them, even given that I now have chemo brain and have found it difficult to concentrate on important stuff. If I am lucky, I will pass. If not, I will have to prepare to do it all over sometime in the future. In the scheme of things, it is definitely not an urgent priority.

My story about chemo will never be pleasant. I really don't buy into the myth that it makes you better, prolongs your life, blah, blah blah. Who says that medication which has the potential to make you infertile, lose your hair, lose your memory, be tired and feel sick to your stomach is a good thing? Who upholds the myth that it is helping you even while robbing you of your genetic makeup, and this is a good thing?

What is wrong with the argument that living just ten good years is better than being robbed of things that are important for the rest of your life? What happened to that argument, the plea for quality of life? People will tell you that they want you to give yourself a chance, they want you around. The thoughts and words are so beautiful, but what happens when you can't have a baby when you want one, or you are so sick, you begin to lose your memory?

I really don't know. As human beings, we tend to have selective memories. You are dealt with bad cards, times goes by, people get on with their lives. Prima facie, that is, at first glance, you get better—and yet you still have to deal with the aftermath of chemo.

My choice of healing suits me just fine. Chemo is an unnecessary evil and I have no proof, no evidence or even guarantee that it is doing any good. I wonder if the supposedly longer life span will be bestowed upon me because I have had chemo.

Plenty of emotional blackmail is involved in chemo. I guess emotional blackmail works when all else fails. Yet I do think it is wrong for anyone to be saddled with that manipulative burden while trying to make an informed decision. When people put chemo treatment and my son in the same sentence it really upset me. I thought it was not fair, even though I know it was said out of love and care for my wellbeing. The decision-making process at the best of times is difficult. No one will knowingly embark on a course that is detrimental to one's health. At least I am certain I wouldn't.

I am glad that I am educated enough, level-headed enough and strong enough to speak out and take some control over my treatment. I cannot thank God enough that I have been in a good place in my own life mentally, physically and emotionally to be able to deal with the challenge I had been presented with. Being at peace and one with the Lord helped.

I don't want anyone who decides to honour me by reading my journal to think that I am one sad, despondent or miserable being. Far from it. I know there is light at end of the tunnel and have always known that. Still, there have been dark times—including those brought on by this chemo—when I lost sight of my faith and hope. Those were the times when the light was dim, like a light bulb that was running out and needed replacing. And as if by a good housekeeper, the bulbs were replaced with brighter and more lasting, durable bulbs.

23 January

I cannot believe my journey is almost coming to any end. On 12 January I told the oncologist about my internet research, and how I had read that having four chemo sessions was as good as having six sessions. I could see she was not impressed with me, but hey ho, my body, my choice. We reached a compromise and agreed I would have four sessions. Really, four sessions. I agreed to have two more sessions of chemo.

I then had my final session on 12 Jan. That was it. I went with all the best intentions to have two more. The breast cancer nurse was pleased with me. We went through the drill: blood counts ok, and so I got prepared for the chemo session.

Now here goes. As I was sitting down, I listened to other patients having chemo. I overheard one individual, a head teacher, say that she was on her fourth chemo session but was beginning to lose her mind and her speech. Jesus H.

Christ! I sat up. I did not need any further convincing. I was no different from the others, but boy oh boy, that helped me make up my mind.

While the nurse was trying to make me feel better, saying, 'Oh, this is your penultimate session,' in my head I was saying 'Goodbye! Never again, I am not coming back here.' I kept that to myself and smiled.

My third and final chemo session was horrendous, the worst to date. Long before I had finished the drip I felt terribly ill. When I got home, things did not get any better. In fact they got progressively worse. I got through it.

In the words of Dr M. Scott Peck, a psychiatrist whose writing I have been reading lately, 'The truth is that our finest moments are most likely to occur when we are feeling deeply uncomfortable, unhappy or unfulfilled. For it is only in such moments, propelled by our discomfort, that we are likely to step out of our rut and start searching for different ways or truer answers.'

I have found my answers. I am not going to be pushed into more treatment I do not want. I am going to make my own choices.

I am not going to be defined by this disease.

30 January

Today I went to Princess Royal for my aromatherapy session. Dee is such a lovely person. Wonderfully, I was able to express myself, telling her exactly how I feel about chemo treatment. It is always nice to speak with someone who reasons on the same wavelength as you. That does not necessarily mean she agreed with everything I said, but we both expressed our opinions about letting nature take care of itself.

After my session I went to see Jane, the breast care nurse, and told her that I am finally done with chemo. I had already taken three chemo sessions too many. Saying this was like a weight being taken off my shoulders.

A few people have asked me if this was the right decision. All I can say in reply is, 'I will never ever know, but I'm glad I made it.'

Nobody knows what will happen in the future. The truth of the matter is it has been the right decision for me here and now. I want to live a better quality of life and not consider the quantity of my life. I am the one who had to be sick, to suffer from terrible headaches and nausea, exhaustion and despair. Nobody else could do it for me. That should give me the absolute power and authority to decide whether I want to continue with the treatment or not. Doctors, nurses, family, friends cannot make that decision. What would have been lovely, though, would have been their support for my decision. I am not asking anyone to agree with me, as it was never their choice to make. I guess if the cancer comes back, I will hear comments like 'She only had three out of six chemo sessions.' I would be very interested in hearing how many people say, 'It is what it is and was meant to be.'

My understanding is that chemo is preventive and not an absolute cure. If it were an absolute cure, then many cancer patients would not have their cancer come back.

To sum up my chemo journey, it was a nightmare, and I have now developed a phobia for the thing called chemotherapy. The mere thought of it makes me want to gag. Worst of all is that I had much more support pre-and post-surgery. I feel I did not have the same support during chemo, which seems rather odd. If anyone should ever ask me, I believe one needs more support during chemo than when undergoing surgery. Chemo and surgery cannot be shared with anyone. You have to undergo these treatments yourself. Yet having people around certainly helps. In my personal and humble opinion, chemo messes with one's head. It is awful and words cannot begin to describe the discomfort, ill ease, pain and suffering one has to endure. I guess people believe or imagine that chemo is far more bearable than it actually is, and as a consequence they leave you on your own. I had many well-wishers the minute I informed them of the diagnosis. But during and after chemo, the well-wishers began to dwindle. I guess to them, the worst was over. There is much more to it than that; I cannot fail to emphasise that cancer, or any chronic illness, is a lonely, personal journey.

I am more than delighted to have my chemo days behind me. I will never undergo any form of chemo ever again in this lifetime—or the next, if you believe in an afterlife or reincarnation.

My personal observation is that more people are scared of surgery than they are of chemo. For my part, I had no fear or reservation with surgery, purely because surgery is more certain for me than chemo. With surgery, if it goes well and is successful that is it. All you have to do after that is get on with the healing process, end of story. Chemo is another matter altogether. It is so terribly uncertain. It messes with your head and upsets your whole system, but for all that you will never know if it has been effective. I suppose one way to measure its success is by the duration you live in remission, without the cancer rearing its ugly head.

1 February

Wow, today would have been another session of chemo. I cannot believe I have really put chemo behind me. I feel elated, walking on air. I am extremely pleased I made the decision to stop and stuck to it. Yeah, good for me. I know I have the capacity to take risks, but I believe not completing the full course of chemo was low risk. For me, it has been all about my belief system, combined with conventional medicine, and I have done what I feel I need to. The future looks bright.

5 February

For the first time in a long time, I finally jogged and power walked again. I felt free. Just me with my bald head, breathing in the crisp, fresh air, being one with nature.

I did not feel any aches or pains after the jogging session. I did not pant or even break out in sweat. In terms of returning to a proper exercise regime, that was encouraging. Today I returned to see Mr Ross, my plastic surgery consultant. It has been exactly four months ago this day that I had my 'tummy tuck and boob job,' in other words, my cancer tumour and calcifications removed and my body rebuilt. Time is a great healer. Today I feel so very well. It is making me appreciate that nothing lasts forever. I cannot but reiterate that it rained for forty days and forty nights, but it did stop raining eventually. My rain has finally stopped. Now it is the right time for my sun shine to come out and shine.

I have drawn on the philosophy and wisdom of the writers of Ecclesiastes, Chapter 13: 'There is a time for everything.' This is my time to laugh. I have cried, I have felt sorrow and pain. But now is the time for me to rejoice. My God has not forsaken me. He did not abandon me; even at my lowest and darkest periods, I have never been alone. My guardian angel and especially the spirit have remained ever so strong. I am grateful of the outcome. Not to mention, I am very pleased that I continued to have my wits around me. All that is left is to have my nipples replaced.

***

My dear friend, you have now read the second part of my journal. As difficult as the cancer diagnosis was, its treatment brought even more unexpected challenges. But I am so happy that I was able to make my own choices and direct the course of my treatment. I resist being considered a 'victim' of cancer. And I persevered, I made it through to the other side.

PHASE THREE: SURVIVAL

It has been one heck of a journey, an experience like nothing I ever expected. Have I learnt anything? One thing I certainly have learnt is how to stay still, the art of not doing anything and not always being in a hurry. Have I learnt tolerance along with patience? I do not know. I hope I have. If not, I have a whole lifetime to continue.

What have I learnt about people? You have the good, the bad and the ugly. People will surprise you, and some will disappoint you. Some people will exceed your expectations, some will overwhelmingly shock you. But however someone approaches you, you have to manage the information that you hear. You have to manage the person, because the person is only acting in the way they know how. But who am I to judge? It is not my place; all I can do is be grateful for the person's time and presence. It is thoughtful of them to be with me, even if I wish some of their words would be better chosen.

My experience has taught me to understand that one should not stress oneself about others. Do your best and leave the rest.

The most important thing I have learnt is that family is terribly important, and they should not be taken for granted. My family have been there for me all the way. I know we can all make choices when it comes to our friends, but with our family it is difficult to make them. Surely it is impossible to abandon another family member when the person is facing a chronic illness. I am so grateful for those bonds.

Another group of people I will never take for granted are my old school mates. Wow! Time does not always help friendship, but it has not touched ours. My old school mates have been with me all the way, even though continents have kept us apart. We have never forgotten our friendship.

The consultant has told me my new nipples are going to be replaced soon. Almost there. Even after four months, it is still rather weird looking at my chest and not have any nipples.

18 February

More thoughts for today: 'When you know how to die, you know how to live.'

'We learn from what hurts us, as much as what loves us.'

Healing is work in progress. I am trying to fill my time, keeping busy. I should say, I have been making a conscious effort to put my cancer experience behind me even whilst appreciating the nature of the ailment.

'Do not depend on the hope of results. You may have to face the fact that your work will apparently be worthless and even achieve no results at all, if not perhaps results opposite to what you expect. As you get to this idea, you start increasingly to concentrate, not on results, but on the value, the rightness, the truth of the work itself. You gradually struggle less and less for an idea and increasingly for specific people. In the end it is the reality of personal relationships that saves everything.'

-Thomas Merton

20 February

I am reading for my assessments, coming up 28 February and 3 March, with my chemo brain. I really do not know why I am putting myself through the assessments, knowing I am not fully healed. I am between a rock and a hard place. I want to do it, but I do not have the same drive, desire and determination after my treatment. However, I want to conclude my Law School experience. Pass or fail, at least I will have completed the assessments and put my best foot forward.

I went to the GP to get my letter for a time extension on the assessments. Having 17 lymph nodes removed from my right side—which hurts most of the time and is always swollen—makes it hard for me to even send text messages. Coupled with a chemo brain, this makes it highly unlikely that I will be able to write and think at the same pace as the rest of the students. Shame.

It is not helping that I am not actually feeling well, and I have been advised that I will need more blood tests.

Annoying. I thought I had hacked this cancer malarkey. Unfortunately for me, that is not the case, and it is not going the way I had planned or hoped.

Nipples

Hello, what is going on here? I ask myself. I have been told that I have been put on a waiting list and it could take another 3–4 months for me to have my nipples replaced. Funny—not!

In the scheme of things I cannot do anything about it, and I really should not complain. I know I will get them replaced one day.

I read a beautiful article about tattoos today. An individual actually had a tattoo in place of a reconstructed bosom after her mastectomy. What an inspired, brilliant idea. I may consider having tattoos where my scars are. I just love people who are capable of thinking outside the box, not just going with the flow for the sake of it. Thank goodness for people like them. Each to their own, that's the life.

***

21 February

Ash Wednesday. Beginning of Lent. From dust we are made unto dust we shall return.

23 February

I am getting through my college work persistently. This means making the best of a bad situation. There is so much to take in, read and understand. It's okay, I am not complaining. I am doing it so I can finally put a closure to my time at Law School. I have invested so much time, effort and energy, not to talk of financial investment. I guess it is only sensible I see it to the end. Pass or fail the assessments, at least I can say I made a good attempt. What more can I do? I keep telling myself this.

I am not sleeping very well, fluctuating between hot and cold. This is not pleasant when all I yearn for is a good night's sleep. It is amazing how my head comes out in beads of sweat at night and is absolutely freezing cold during the day. Side effects of that silly thing called chemo.

After reading Lightning, I remember going to the office and telling one of my friends about the novel and what it says about chemotherapy. She found it hilarious, and reassured me it was just a book. That there was no way chemotherapy could be so bad. Hmm, really?

Now, I think Danielle Steel's book was quite honest, and her book prepared me for the worst. At the time I read it I really thought I would not be having chemo. In fact, I had convinced myself I would not be having it.

Chemo does not do what it says on the tin. If it did, then cancer would not reoccur. Ahh, that is my personal opinion. I am not scientifically trained, only a receiver of horrible stuff. I know people will insist that it does help. No one can actually guarantee a complete cure with chemo. What I say then is, why bother? Who is interested in prolonging life for the sake of it? One has to have a jolly good reason!

That does not make me a disbeliever, because I really get fed up of people trying to tell me I have to believe. I have plenty of faith, but my personal relationship with my God is a personal one. I do not have to scream from the hilltops or impose my personal convictions on anyone. It is not my way of doing things. Neither do I have to pass judgement on those who wish to do that. People have to do what makes them comfortable, as long as it does not interfere with others who do not want it. One size does not necessarily fit all. We are all seeking happiness. Recommendations can be made about what might make another happy, but it is all subjective, trial and error approach. Maybe one day a formula for happiness will be found. That will sell really, really well. But this seems unlikely. Happiness is subjective and never lasting. The same could perhaps be said of health.

Oh, I have to go back to work on 2 April. This is purely for financial reasons. I cannot live on half-pay for more than one month. Even that month is going to be inconvenient and uncomfortable. But who can I turn to? Who will help me out? I have to muster the energy to ring the cancer number and see if I can get any help. Lord have mercy. Cancer is so not easy.

I believe strongly two good heads are so much better than one, no matter what. Sometimes it is not always about the money. It is about sharing your thoughts, having someone to lift you up when you are having a bad day, someone to laugh with you when you are having a good day, to accompany you on a walk, to watch TV. Ultimately, just to laugh and cry together. That is what two good friends do. It is a real shame I am on my own right now. Not desired, but what can I do?

I am trawling through my college work, wishing I were far away, lazing around, having fun and living it up. Alas, not for me right now.

25 February

Sitting in front of my computer with my Criminal Law books in front of me. Hmm, will get back to those later. Tiring. My chemo brain is not working, oh dear!

I have decided to take a step back today and review my cancer experience, review the decisions I made with regard to my treatment. I did some further research and realise I am terribly pleased with the choices I have made and would not change a thing. My reading uncovered a few more surprises. Despite all that I have read regarding breast cancer, I am learning more with each passing day. Education and knowledge is fluid, we can always learn something new. One should never tire trying to learn. Most of all, I am learning on the emotional front. I am learning that my actions and reactions are pretty normal. I am beginning to understand that my not being melodramatic about my illness is purely down to the way I have handled it. I started writing my journal from the outset. In my reading, I have learnt that writing in a journal increases well-being and reduces infections according to the latest research. I did not know that.

On the whole, I think I have been able to reduce my stress levels by writing in my journal. Having said that, all is not well. I am suffering from these hot flashes at night. In fact, I may be going through menopause—another side effect of chemo. Oh, for goodness' sake! I am trying to get my head around the benefit of this horrible thing they call chemo.

If I am not suffering from menopause, then my symptoms of fatigue, etc. can only mean one thing: Cancer:

the return. I think it is highly unlikely. Still, research suggests that cancer returns within two or three years, but breast cancer can reoccur anytime. So having breast cancer could be life sentence. You have to live the rest of your natural life knowing it could come back to visit you. What a wonderful thought. That is what research says. Too much information on the internet. Hey ho, you do not allow yourself to get bogged down with that type of information, because the truth is when your number is up, there is nothing you can say or do that will stop the good Lord himself from taking you back to Him. Our Father in Heaven has allocated us a time and a spot to go do our part. We are all actors and the world is our stage. It is up to us to perform our part brilliantly until it is cut from the script, until we are made redundant on Earth and reemployed in Heaven. In the meantime, enjoy life, live it to the full and do not worry too much.

We come here with nothing and will go back with nothing.

The fact remains, I have tried to hold it together without falling to bits, and this has maybe given a false impression of my own wellness.

I am not a saint, not perfect—far from it—but I have been through a horrible, rough, interesting, traumatic experience. That cannot be taken away from me. The fact that I gave up chemotherapy and decided to embark on my studies does not mean that I am not hurting. The fact that I am not openly weeping and openly being a pain and feeling sorry for myself does not mean I am not feeling hurt and lonely. I have found the whole experience an extremely lonely one. I am not strong, I am actually weak, even though I cannot afford to show it. But I know that this is my journey and it is down to me to make it interesting. For every day that goes by, I cannot get these hours back, so it is up to me to live each day and appreciate the beauty it contains: the sunshine, the rain, the cold. It is not for me to whinge for the sake of it. I am too busy thinking how I can improve the quality of my life.

My spirit is strong, it has remained strong for a long time. My faith is strong and I believe we all have to respect each other's faith and beliefs. We all have our own way of relating to our maker. There is no script or known formulae for how we should or can do this. All we have are the recommendations as laid down in holy books. That does not mean, either, that the holy books and their recommendations are good for everyone.

As for me, I just have to get on with my life. I will book my holiday, I will go away for a while and rethink my life, trying to find a winning formula. I will put a closure to certain things. I will try to do more enjoyable things, including those that give me the most pleasure. Life is always in a state of flux—fluid, always in a state of change. I will continue to strive to have an open mind, embrace the new and hold on to all that is good and old.

Let's hope the cancer does not return to soon. It will be good to have a break from hospitals, treatment and generally feeling unwell. Right now I am just okay. Not 100%, but considering where I have been, where I am coming from, even 40% is good.

I will resume my jogging in earnest and continue to keep fit, eat healthy. That will not change.

Yeah, my hair is beginning to grow back. It hurts; my entire head hurts. The texture is different and the colour of the hair coming back is silver.

My discoloured finger- and toe-nails are beginning to return to their normal colour. So that is all good. My body, mysterious thing, is repairing itself. All it needs is time.

11 March

Wow!!! I cannot believe how time flies. I wonder why I have not written for a while now. I have missed my precious journal.

I have been busy studying for my Property and Civil/Criminal Litigation assessments, including Advocacy, which I attended yesterday. I cannot believe I actually sat the assessments. It was a feat of mind over matter. If I did not mind, then it would not matter. Amazing.

It was truly an interesting experience. One lesson I have learnt is that with patience, perseverance and being surrounded by the right people, anything is possible.

I stayed close to my Law School College mates. They encouraged me big time and ensured I did not give up. They did not put up with any of my excuses. I tried to come up with every excuse in the book not to continue with the course. I woke up one day after giving up on chemo and realized that I had to carry on. I had to justify why I gave up chemo (to myself and nobody else). I had to show how much I could do. Not only that, giving up chemo put me in another place, another phase of my cancer journey.

I have now shifted from being a cancer sufferer to a cancer survivor, one living with cancer. The operative word is living. My theory is if you are a survivor, you have to get on with life. You owe it to yourself to get on with life.

In my case, I have to pick up some of the pieces from where I left off. I am not in a fortunate position at this time, not a good place from which to drastically alter or change my lifestyle, owing to the life-threatening ailment.

Nothing stopped, nobody stopped because I had cancer, and rightly so. Life carried on for each one of us. That said, not only did nobody stop, but some people seemed downright unwilling to slow down and see how I was doing, or to think how they could be helpful in their speech or actions. In some cases, the words I've heard were painful, but life is like that. If we have no knowledge or understanding of a situation, we can be mindless, thoughtless in our words and actions. And yet others do care, and show it. A dear friend of mine, Muobo, said that she did not know about the ailment, but decided to go on the internet and read about it so she could understand what I am going through. That was touching and moving. In many instances I was treated with compassion and consideration. Of course, the college I was attending, BPP College of Law Holborn, has special needs officer and invigilators who showed me the true meaning of compassion, understanding and sympathy. I guess we would not expect anything less from lawyers who know the law. I fulfilled the criteria to sit my exams—under special needs conditions, that goes without saying. It was the encouragement and compassion that certain individuals extended to me that made all the difference.

    I put my best foot forward and gave the assessment my best shot. I put in 110%. I remained focused and determined. All I can do now is wait for the outcome. Pass or fail or re-sit the assessments, each possibility is okay. I proved to myself that I am alive, surviving if not thriving yet.

    I did not let the side effects of chemo get in the way of the assessments, I did not let the numbness in my right hand deter me from writing. Honestly, I thought I was writing fast! Or so it seemed. I did not realise how slow I was. Writing fast was a figment of my imagination. I did not let my slight memory loss keep me from remembering as much as I possibly could. I worked really hard. I had to teach myself a lot, as I had missed a number of lectures and tutorials. It was hard, it took a lot out of me. I lost reading days out of sheer exhaustion. I pushed my mental and physical capacity to the limits. Sitting down for hours on end was not good for my abdomen. I still had bandages on my stomach and chest. I was extremely exhausted at the end of it, but it was worth every minute. I did it! I did it! I got through it.

The key is: when you want to do something, nothing and or nobody can really stop you. It has a lot to do with self-worth, self-belief and possibly confidence in one's ability. I did not have confidence that I will pass the assessments. But I was confident that I would be present at the exam centre on the day to sit and write the assessment no matter what. Much mental preparation and planning went into it. Especially, we had to plan my coming off chemo, having time to recuperate sufficiently from the immediate side effects, time to read without it being excessively discomforting.

The assessments took me away from thinking too much or even dwelling on the ailment. Having said that, I am a strong believer that we all have the capacity to survive, albeit in our own way. The strategy and method I adopted worked for me, but may not work for someone else. In any event, our priorities differ. Yet we all could handle adverse situations.

Difficulties are a part of life and living. There is a time for everything under the sun. The cancer for me has been challenging, but more challenging has been the roller coaster of emotions.

My studies were a means of escapism, and they worked.

11 March

Spring has sprung. What a glorious day. The sun is lovely, shining outside and in my heart. The weather does affect the way we feel and behave.

Today may be the first day of my new life. Six months down the line, I can say that I really have moved from being a cancer sufferer to a cancer survivor.

It is a known fact that one cannot, or really does not, get the all-clear. None of us knows for sure. Medicine can only do so much. Doctors are human and they can only tell you so much. At the end of the day it is down to you to take ownership and responsibility for your life including, health and your general wellbeing.

Luckily for me, I have survived. During the cancer treatment phase, I made a conscious effort to look good, to be well groomed when I went out. I chose to dress well, to carry myself well, to do as much physical exercise by walking and mental exercise by reading as I could. I tried to remain as positive as I could. It was not easy and each minute was different. I slept when I could sleep, I ate the good foods—vegetables, fruits and protein. I began to treat my body as a temple and give it the respect that it truly deserved. It is my body, after all. If I did not look after it, who else would?

I tried to look after my mind; I read books, magazines. None of it came easy but I did not give up on my self-motivation. I owed it to myself to do it and I did.

When you have nobody or no one to motivate you on an interesting journey like this, you have to dig deep, very deep. Instinctively, your survival mechanism sets in, your sense of self-worth keeps you going. For as long as you are on Earth, you will get by so long as you realise nobody owes you anything and you owe nobody anything. The more you are aware of this, the easier it is to carry on healing mind, body and soul.

I had good friends who walked with me on my journey. At the start, loads of friends accompanied me, but as with anything else in life some fell by the wayside. They had to fulfil other needs. And some are still walking with me.

I went jogging yesterday, taking advantage of this wonderful weather. I just love the outdoors. I feel free and exhilarated when I am surrounded by nature.

Home life is good. The boys are doing well. My little one is maturing. What more can I possibly ask for? I have to appreciate the immediate present and plan for the future. With God all things are possible. Something good has to come out of what has happened in recent months. At times I feel I have been inadequate, out of my depth, even as I try to ensure that the boys and home life remains stable and constant.

April 3

After five long months, I have finally returned to work. It is a joy to be back. At least it will keep me occupied and stop my thoughts from wandering to dark places. As they say, 'the idle mind is a playground for the devil.'

Things are beginning to look up, and I can only move forward. Life is interesting and we never know what to expect from one day to another. I smile, because life can be extremely exciting and wonderful. All we have to do is occasionally think outside the box and embrace what is good and bad.

As a cancer survivor, and one who will be living with cancer, I can now concentrate on living my life to the fullest.

First things first: I have finally booked a holiday. I am going to Washington, DC to see my friend Risi and her young baby Tobi. I am also going to see my cousin, Demola, in New Jersey on 13 April. I intend to enjoy every minute of it. That is something for me to look forward to.

Easter is coming, another break to look forward to with Ayulie and Jnr. Jnr, Ayulie and I have been going jogging together. Absolutely brilliant. I have been coming last—shame, but it has also been great team work and family fun. I am delighted I can do that with my boys. It also shows that I am getting stronger, fitter and healthier. I am making the right food choices. I don't need too much food to survive; I don't want to ruin my 'tummy tuck.' I simply love my new flat tummy, and am not in a hurry to ruin the look by eating too much or the wrong foods.

Am I vain or what? Hahaha, I love it!

Speaking of vanity, I still have not got my nipples back. When I rang the hospital, I learned that I am still on the waiting list, which takes about 24 weeks. I am not going to moan about that at all, because the NHS saved my life. They delivered when they had to. My nipples are not a priority; there must be someone out there with more urgent and pressing needs than nipple replacement. I will wait patiently until my turn comes. Luckily, I am not in a relationship, so I don't have to deal with that side of things. Even if I get in a relationship, the individual will have to accept me with or without nipples in the meantime. Like my cancer, I will not be defined by my nipples. There is so much more to me than nipples.

College has been great. It keeps me busy and gives me a sense of purpose. I passed my solicitors accounts. This makes me very proud of myself, as I sat the assessment in between chemo sessions. What more can I say? I hope to God I pass the assessments I sat in Feb/March. It will definitely help my morale.

I went to visit my dear friends Foster, Charlotte and kids in Witham. It was another beautiful day. As I drove down with Ayulie and Jnr, we took in the scenery. I relied heavily on my Sat Nav. The boys were great. Had a pleasant afternoon at Foster's. It was a great opportunity for me to thank him for our friendship and thank them for all their moral support while I was a cancer sufferer.

My friends and family have helped me so much. The phone calls, cards, presents and their presence have pulled me through.

I am working really, really hard to remain positive. I am under no illusions that my journey has ended.

But I am going to enjoy the ride.

Epilogue

Many years later, I am still alive. The healing process has been slow yet steady. It has taken me these years to get to where I am today.

My cancer has not returned. However, that does not stop me from wondering every day if it will ever come back. I try not to let those thoughts rule my life, even though it is hard not to think about. It comes with the territory.

I am faced with the constant reminder from my scars that I am a survivor. My scars hurt constantly. I have learnt to live with the pain.

I did not pass my Legal Practice Course (LPC). I did not pass a couple of assessments, and I needed to pass all my assessments to get my certificate. But it was to be expected, given what I was up against. I needed to put a closure to it, and while the closure was not one that I wanted, it was one that I have come to live with. It's okay. I tried my best; that is all I could do with the cards I had been dealt.

I have learnt to be more patient, understanding and tolerant. I have learnt to let go of things I believe I need or want. I can do without a lot of things, because none of these things will matter when your health is being challenged.

I have also learnt that one cannot underestimate the strength we have to face our challenges.

Most importantly, each day is different. When we think we have lost something, we do not realise that we have actually gained something else.

What I have learnt is that living with cancer is a lifetime commitment. Adopting a holistic approach, ensuring that mind, body and soul are in perfect harmony, will go a very long way.

I have learnt that cancer can have a devastating impact on finances. It is ever so difficult to discuss finances as a newly diagnosed cancer patient, but I have learnt that it is a part of the healing process. Try not to be upset or hurt if a nurse tries to open up a discussion relating to work and finances. A lot of us believe that we need to go through treatment first and then tackle other issues. I have learnt that is not necessarily the most practical way to go about it.

We do have the capacity and ability as homo sapiens to deal with more than one issue at a time, no matter how painful.

The hardest lesson after all these years is knowing that being diagnosed with cancer and going through treatment was actually the easiest part. The hardest part for me is survivorship. Life goes on. I was not prepared for the long-term effects of treatment. At some point I lost my speech; I began to stammer. To this day I stammer when I am terribly upset or get into an argument. It hurts, because I never stammered prior to chemotherapy.

I have had to look for work, I have had to dream other dreams that I hope I can realise over time.

While some dreams have been lost in my life, others have been realised.

I continually try to improve my lot, to be the best person that I can with the tools I have to work with. I try to be nothing more than my true, authentic self.

It has been said and it is true: cancer changes a person. Cancer has changed me and I hope for the best.

In my journal entries, I have mentioned my very strong yearning to travel.

I did not understand why my desire to travel was so strong. However, as I begun to heal, in the early days I joined several groups. At a Macmillan sponsored workshop, where survivors shared their fears, goals and aspirations, my feelings suddenly became clearer. The survivors who spoke talked about their desire to travel the world; some had been given a time limit to live, some other participants were going through their second and third bout of battling a cancer diagnosis. The common theme was the need to travel. All of a sudden I felt normal. I began to understand that my feelings came with the terrain.

I was physically fragile, but more psychologically fragile than I knew. I made some decisions that in hindsight I would not have if I understand what I was doing.

I returned back to work, but I did not have the support there to enable me continue working. When I returned, I was expected to carry on as though nothing had happened to me. It was a tough call. I had not recovered from the chemotherapy and surgery. I had bandages on my abdomen and plasters where my nipples had yet to be constructed.

The area of Property Management that I work in—Leasehold Management—is a specialist area and not understood by many owing to the complex legislation surrounding it. Thus my presence and continued work was important to my employers. My health was important to me, so there was a conflict. I tried my best possible to carry on with my duties and heal at the same time because I was still under no illusion about how much I needed this job to sustain my income, but in the end I did not succeed.

I worked twice as hard to prove that I was the same person after my diagnosis and treatment. The strain took its toll on me and my health.

Needless to say, at some point we had to go separate ways. My employers did not know how to deal with a cancer diagnosis. All they could see was the long-term absences from the office.

I recall that the situation hastened my departure did not sit well with me. But I was extremely mindful that if I had to take any action whatsoever, I had to be strong. If you decide to take on an organization you have to have the support and toe the line.

I know I sat with tears flowing down my cheeks, talking to the child in me, saying, 'How can you take on the organization? You know what is happening is not right, but how will you get to work? You will have to adhere to all the rules and regulations, get nothing wrong, be at work on time. Are you strong enough to do that?'

The child in me knew it was virtually impossible to do so. My decision was to let it go and focus my energies on healing.

My colleague Rosemary had been diagnosed with lung cancer and then breast cancer. I vividly remember when she had been newly diagnosed with lung cancer. She came to work and I asked her why she was there. She replied, 'Alero, I have to pay my mortgage'. I did not get it (I had not been diagnosed at the time). All I could see was a colleague who was unwell continuing to come to work.

Rosemary became my mentor when I was diagnosed. She told me about chemo and said 'Alero, chemo gets progressively worse with each session.' She was right. She also let me know that our employers and colleagues were not as well informed about cancer survivors and work. Rosemary was a manager in the organization. She had her own office. On her return to work after being diagnosed with breast cancer, she was put in the corner of an open-plan office and made invisible.

I am not suggesting in any manner, shape or form whether our employers were right or wrong. For all I know it was a mutual agreement and done for Rosemary's well-being. I narrate this from a spectator's point of view. Yet it is amazing what we take in without being aware of the impact it may have on us.

I had not been diagnosed at the time so I was not in a position to suggest any of that was going to happen to me. It did not happen to me.

Rosemary finally passed away from her cancer. She fought a good fight. Ironically, Rosemary was in a hospice very near my home, so I was a frequent visitor until she died. Rosemary's last words to me—and I hear them all the time: 'Alero, you did not finish your chemo sessions and you are here today. Did I do the right thing to continue to take chemo?'

I replied, 'You did the right thing for you, and that is all that matters.'

She also told me that even though she was going to church she had lost her faith, but she did not want anyone to know. I got it; I understood her and I empathized with her.

My cousin Buge was diagnosed in 2009; she was self-employed and had her son to fend for. She worried constantly about her finances. She lost her fight against cancer in 2012. One of her biggest concerns was for her young son. My heart reaches out to him and my thoughts are always with Buge, who is resting in peace. I stumbled across a former colleague, Sylvana, on one of my numerous outpatient visits with my plastic surgeon. She told me she had been diagnosed with breast cancer. Even at that stage her primary concern was that she was self-employed and didn't know how she would keep up with her mortgage repayments; she also had a young daughter to care for. Sylvana did not make it; she also lost her battle to unexplainable silent killer.

I narrate these stories because it is stories like these, including my own, that led me to become a Macmillan Cancer Voice and an advocate. I was confused, angry, upset. What was it about cancer that scared employers? Is it the uncertainty of the illness?

As I began to heal, I continued to ponder, until one day I saw an advertisement from Macmillan Cancer Support looking for patients to sit on a panel to examine survivorship and work. I submitted my application, giving all the reasons why I felt I was a suitable survivor to sit on the panel. I was selected and my journey on becoming an active cancer campaigner and advocate truly began.

On that panel I met the distinguished Dr Gail Eva, who works on vocational rehabilitation for people with cancer. In the process of getting to know each other, I asked Dr Eva why she does what she does. She explained to me that if we break our bones, we are given extensive rehabilitation. What she did not understand is why cancer patients are not given the same form of rehabilitation, given the fact that cancer is equally as traumatic and disabling as any physical illness. We take almost the same amount of time off work to heal, but we do not have same amount of rehabilitation as people with visible disabilities.

Dr Eva asked what motivated me, and I told her my story in brief and my passion about cancer and work. The conversation took place four years ago. To this day Dr Eva and I still work together, doing our bit to help academic researchers, nurses, employers and stakeholders, including members of parliament, to understand the impact that work has on the survivorship of cancer survivors.

Academic researchers like Dr Gail Eva are invaluable to us.

I've mentioned that when I was diagnosed I was naïve; I did not have an understanding of cancer. It was alien. What on earth was this scary thing that proved such a silent killer?

My father (may his soul rest in perfect peace) told me that no one can take your knowledge away from you. He also taught me that knowledge is power. I will never forget my father's emphasis and passion for me to learn, to educate my mind. My father never ever joked with the education of his children. He strongly believed if he had nothing to leave for in way of inheritance he would ensure that his children received a sound education. That is the legacy my father left me—a platform to education.

Based on that legacy, I started my knowledge journey to know more about cancer. My first port of call was to apply for a place called Project LEAD. The Project LEAD Institute is a six-day intensive science course for breast cancer advocates covering the basics of cancer biology, genetics, epidemiology, research design and advocacy. The course provides a foundation of scientific knowledge upon which participants can strengthen and empower themselves as activists.

Project LEAD is an American non-profit organization. I was offered a place as an international advocate. My training took place in Cancun, Mexico. It was one of the most amazing training courses I have been on. It was definitely intense, but being surrounded by survivors from all over the world looking for answers on how to eradicate breast cancer made the intensity of the course pale in comparison.

I returned to the UK with a better understanding of breast cancer and was more equipped to be a better advocate. My thirst for knowledge, for understanding my cancer, had enabled me to empower myself. I learned about the rights of cancer patients and about treatment options. One of the most important things that came through in my lessons is the importance of diet and exercise. These things have a critical impact on our health throughout our lives.

I have attended Macmillan Support cancer conferences in the UK and the San Antonio Breast Cancer Symposium in Texas, USA. The Symposium is designed to provide state-of-the-art information on the experimental biology, etiology, prevention, diagnosis and therapy of breast cancer and premalignant breast disease to an international audience of academic and private physicians and researchers. The knowledge that I have acquired in my quest to understand cancer has served me well as I continue in my role as a patient advocate, consultant, trainer and advisor.

One of the researchers I work with asked me, 'Alero, what motivates people like you to talk to academic researchers, to share your story'?

I have never asked myself that question. I know I did not realise my dreams snatched away by my cancer. But I do know I did not lose my voice. I do know I survived, and surely there has to be a reason why some of us survive and some of us do not make it. We are all gifted with different talents and I recognize I have the ability to speak. I am using my vocal cords to deliver a message and that message is we all need to come together to eradicate cancer and all other critical illnesses. If I could sing I guess I would have conveyed the same message in music, and if I could draw I would have conveyed my message in my art.

My art form is my voice, and that is what motivates me. I pray I am heard and listened to. Let me be a voice for those who are yet to find their voices or other ways of expressing themselves.

I am in awe of academic researchers who through their research look for ways to find a solution to a worldwide health problem. Their talent and gift is the ability to conduct research.

I am able to write today as a consumer of past research. If cancer survivors before me did not speak out, presumably

I would not be here today to speak, write and share my experience.

Today, I am in work. It has not been an easy journey finding employment after a critical illness. I found it very difficult to put on application forms that I suffered a critical illness, for several reasons. At the time, the UK and the rest of the world were going through a recession. I did not want to limit my chances of being shortlisted for an interview not to talk of being offered a job.

And again, somewhere in my subconscious I felt ashamed to even say I had cancer. I don't know what happened or where it came from, but the shame happened, especially when I was in work. I had to work so hard even when I was feeling unwell. At some point I decided to take time off to heal properly, as I had kept going and was not healing properly.

It took a 23-year-old fellow cancer survivor to release me from my guilt and shame. I was registering with a recruitment agency. On my CV, I had a gap where I was off work healing. The consultant asked, me why the gap? I wanted the ground to swallow me up. Despite my numerous years of work experience he wanted an explanation. At that point I decided to tell him that I was a cancer survivor who had time off work in order to heal. It did not faze him. Instead, he explained to me that he was also a survivor, having had cancer as a child up until he was 18. We exchanged notes and he told me I should never hide the fact that I am a survivor, that I will be amazed how understanding employers can be if they really want you and your experience. It was a revelation. I told him it was easy for him to say, he was young. He quickly shut me up and said I should not give him excuses.

When I left that meeting I was a changed person. Thanks to him, at the next job interview when I was asked about the gap in my CV, I took the plunge and said, 'I am a cancer survivor, I had to take time out to heal.'

The interviewers did not bat an eyelid, but told me I was strong to come out the other end. Needless to say, I got the job.

In my journal I stress that life continues and does not stop because of a cancer diagnosis.

My life has not stopped and my challenges have not stopped. In September 2012 the block where I have an apartment was involved in a fire incident and I was rendered homeless for twelve months. Barely three weeks after the fire incident I lost a contract. Life could not have been worse. But guess what? I was sad, upset and thought *how unfair*! in one breath, yet in another breath I was upbeat and happy and hopeful. Why? Because nothing could be as challenging as going through cancer. I was equipped to deal with yet another setback—and it was a setback. These were things that happened outside my control. I could not prevent those events from happening. I felt the gods were having a laugh at my expense.

Through it all, I am still a mother, sister, friend, daughter, auntie and colleague, but more importantly, a cancer voice.

The good news is I have nipples! During the breast reconstruction a part of the skin is tucked in and marked out. That is the part that will be used to reconstruct nipples.

I had my new nipples in the spring of 2007. It was a simple procedure. I went in as a day patient. After I was given a local anaesthetic, the skin that had been tucked in was moulded into a nipple. A couple of months later I went back to have tattooing done to form the areola, the pigmented area around the nipple.

The reason for the procedure was to make my newly reconstructed bosom look as real as humanly possible.

The tattooing procedure was very painful. I was not given a local anaesthetic and it simply hurt.

To anyone reading, cancer should not be underestimated. It is not a pleasant illness, hence it has many faces. Diagnosis and treatment are merely physical symptoms. The emotional and financial impact should not be ignored.

No cancer is easy, irrespective of the brave fronts we all put on to save our loved ones from worrying more than they should.

Surviving cancer is forever.

It has been a very interesting journey. A journey I wish I did not have to make, but a journey I have and will continue to make.

I cannot wait for the day we are told cancer has been eradicated for good.

In the meantime, may we all find the strength to love each other and care for each other in good times and not so good times.

P.S. I now have a significant other in my life. Wow!

Ayulie's Story

I can vividly remember first hearing about my mother's diagnosis in my Auntie's car, on the way back home. As soon as she revealed that she had been diagnosed with breast cancer, my first reaction was to put my jumper over my head and cry; presumably this being because, as a young and naïve teenager, I instantly associated the word 'cancer' with death.

A few weeks after the diagnosis, my mother was operated on and then began her road to recovery. When my mother first arrived back home it took me a while to digest witnessing her body transformation, seeing as she underwent a double mastectomy. Part of me was intrigued, while another part had difficulty in registering such an alteration (maybe I felt that this was a permanent reminder that cancer had 'changed' my mum).

I'm partially grateful my mother's ordeal occurred at a time when I was still in school. Fortunately, this provided a much needed escape from the harsh realities that faced my mother. With everything coming as quite of a shock to me, I can remember confiding in my friends about what occurred. I'm extremely fortunate that they were supportive and caring about the situation. To this day, they still ask about the well-being of my mother and how she is coping.

***

Junior's Story

Upon meeting and getting to knowing this amazingly kind woman, who had just accepted me as one of her own, for the first time, my 16-year-old mind was constantly puzzled, even crippled with confusion. How she could be so unwell and yet so normal on the surface? Would I be losing a mother if things didn't go well?

It was all going by too quickly for me. One moment, I am getting used to calling this woman 'Mother,' and the next I am in hospital with her family seeing her go off to surgery. I was very scared for her, but I knew my emotions couldn't compare to that of her immediate family, who were crying profusely.

I remember our visit post-surgery and the relief we all felt that she survived, that she had crossed one hurdle in the journey to better health. I kept thinking that God couldn't have given me this chance and new family only to take her away from me immediately. This gave me comfort and assurance that whatever happened, she would survive.

A quick fast forward to a few weeks after Mum had started chemo: I came back home from school one afternoon and the house was quiet. No Mum sitting on the couch watching TV, no smell of rice and stew coming from the kitchen. Nothing. Gripped with panic, I went straight to her bedroom. There I found her, lying still in bed. I went to her side and asked if she needed anything. She said she was okay. I always admired her self-sufficiency and ability to see to the needs of her children while battling this illness. She seemed to do it all with ease. That afternoon, I proceeded anyways to juice her a lemon drink, as I knew she always enjoyed these during her bad days. I would also add a pinch of sugar even though she asked me not to. I couldn't understand how she could drink it with all that tartness. When she would call me out on it softly, I would deny adding the sugar. I wanted to do everything to make her happy, and a sweet drink to me was better than a sour one.

The hardest part, I remember, was the nausea. I would rub her back as she let it all out, wishing I could do anything to ease the pain. I would wake up in the night and go by her door and listen to see if she was awake and in pain. It was traumatic for me, and I remember thinking this must be even more traumatic for her son, my brother Ayulie. With it all, I constantly prayed and hoped that she would get better and we all could move on.

Looking back, it is interesting to see the damages cancer and the treatment process do to a person. After Mum left her job and her primary focus became managing treatment and getting better, I noticed the changes in her moods. There were many ups and down during her journey and I remember being very confused about her health. *Is this normal? Does this mean she's not getting better? Will it ever stop? Will she ever be the same after it's all done?* These were the questions I was always pondering.

Through it all, Mum always managed to stay on top of her duties. She always found the strength to make food for Ayulie and me. She was always on top of our schoolwork and made sure we were getting on well at school and with our peers. She never failed or gave up on her motherly duties.

Her whole world was collapsing so fast, and she honestly couldn't do anything but be strong and to carry on the best way she knew how.

Yes, cancer does change the lives of its victims and those around them. I choose to believe that Mum had to go through it for a reason, and she has come out a stronger individual. I am grateful for her strength and ability to pick up where she left off as soon as she was better. With many opportunities lost, many new ones have come and many will continue to come. I am forever thankful for her life and having her in mine and will forever love and cherish every moment I have with her.

***

Demi's Story

It's my time to address the elephant in the room

Not being a writer, when my auntie kindly approached me to write about her cancer for a section in her book and I immediately agreed, I was ignoring the fact that I suffer greatly from articulately expressing myself on paper—so please don't judge my efforts too harshly. Initially, I informed her that I would not be able to write something straight away because I was preoccupied with other priorities, but I assured her that I would swiftly have my writing completed and sent to her in a matter of days. Unfortunately, those days turned into weeks and those weeks turned into months and still I had produced nothing. Even with gentle reminders, I left my auntie patiently waiting for the writing that I had promised her. On the occasions where I remembered that this was something that I needed to do, I would proceed with my brainstorming by attempting to recall every single detail about that period of time. However; something quickly dawned on me, and that something was further consolidated when my friends asked what I remembered about the time in which my auntie had cancer. The answer to their question was *very little*. By *very little*, it means the point that I could not even definitively tell you the year in which she was diagnosed with cancer.

My friends had been asking me about my experience of cancer in my family, because one of our best friend's mums had recently had her cancer return and at the time there was a possibility that it could be terminal. On recollection a few days afterwards, I finally realised that my trouble writing stemmed from more than a lack of time; it was more a lack of figuring out something substantial to write which had caused me to continuously push the task to the side. One would've thought that my main difficulty would be trying to remember the hurtful and depressing memories of such a traumatic time. Yet I'm sure many people who have been through traumatising situations will relate when I say that only upon attempting to access those memories did I realise that I had subconsciously and unwittingly repressed most of them. I knew that repression happens to people, as I had seen about it on the television and read about it. However, it is hard to comprehend that the brain can adopt such a dramatic coping mechanism as essentially wiping out or fragmenting memories that should have a strong imprint in your mind. It's especially perplexing given that I can still vividly remember some embarrassing and what I would consider traumatic moments which I wouldn't mind repressing. Obviously age is a factor, and when I think hard, I'm sure some of the gaps in my memory are due to my not even knowing what was going on in the first place. So now that I have laboured on about how little I remember, if I were to have written this piece as a recollection of the time from my point of view, it would probably be very succinct:

My aunt felt a lump on her breast, so she went to the GP. The GP recommended her to a breast cancer specialist at Princess Royal Hospital. The specialist took mammograms and they confirmed that there was a lump and that it was cancerous. We were very sad and we cried about it. My aunt then had to go for surgery at St Thomas' Hospital (it could've been Guy's but I don't quite remember) and she had to have a double bilateral mastectomy. She was in the hospital for a while and she had to take chemotherapy and that made her ill. But then eventually she got better.

Now I won't lie. When I try harder, more bits and pieces do come back to me. For instance, I hadn't used the term 'double bilateral mastectomy' in years, yet I could reel it off straight from the top of my head.

That being said, I don't think there would be much to gain from powering through the facts and I personally want to write about something different. What I want to write about is a prominent theme that most people who have suffered from or know someone who has suffered from cancer or any life-threatening illness will probably know all too well, and that theme is *time*. It came to me while I was in the shower thinking to myself that I didn't really have the *time* to write this, and again as I was discussing with my group of friends why our friend wasn't spending more *time* with her mum who has cancer. For me, this really summed up my underlying experience with cancer.

Naturally, when you see a loved one suffering you are saddened by the pain they are going through and that can strongly affect you. But based on my experience, what hurts most is when you start to think about the different aspects of *time* associated with the cancer. When your loved one is a diagnosed with cancer, the first and most heart-breaking thing you think is that they could potentially die soon and how much *time* you have left with them. While my aunt was in surgery the whole *time* was spent worrying about how the surgery was going and if she'd make it out okay and if it would be successful. When you have *time* to come to terms with the realisation that cancer is real, not just something we see in the media, and that it can personally affect you just as much as the next person and you just have to deal with it, your thoughts turn to how you can use the *time* that you have left with your loved one because you don't know if you have two days, two years or twenty years. You become so much more aware of *time* that it's actually scary to think about. Will they recover? How long will it take if they do? If only we could turn back *time* and make it so that things were different. These are questions that undoubtedly ran through my mind and I'm sure the minds of many. I remember fairly recently being at the funeral of one of my mum's and aunt's close childhood friends who passed away due to breast cancer. I looked at my mum as she had tears running down her face behind her sunglasses.

'Why didn't I get to spend more *time* with her before she passed away?' she wept. We really don't realise how precious *time* is until it becomes threatened, and most of the time we don't realise how much or rather how little *time* we have left until it's gone.

For me, being able to see my aunt happy and healthy today is something that I shouldn't but do still take for granted, because not so long ago I wasn't in this position. The whole experience with cancer has made me become regularly thankful for the good health of myself and everyone around me, and every day I acknowledge how blessed I am to have people around me that love and support me and look after me when I am in need. With that being said, I am very grateful that my aunt asked me to write this, because in doing so the process has helped me to identify that I do still take *time* for granted and I know I am probably not alone in that, especially with the pleas that are constantly made to my cousin to spend more *time* with my aunt. When my aunt was going through the main stages of her cancer I was way too young to fully comprehend the situation. Nevertheless, reassessing it now that I am older and wiser has allowed me to gain a new and freshened perspective on what was until recently only a repressed memory, and I am certain that this has now changed my future outlook on how I live my life and manage my *time*, for the better.

***

Risi's story

My girlfriend, my dear Alero.

I don't know where to start. I suppose it was seeing you in that hospital bed that really shocked me. Tears stung my eyes and I could hardly see. I did not have the heart to tell you how I had already passed your bed and did not recognize you. The woman that I had caught a glimpse of lying in that bed by the window had looked bloated and lifeless. I had felt so sorry for her and tried to avoid any eye contact. Then, when I could not find you, I went to the nurse on the ward and asked for you and she said 'You have just walked by her.' You were that woman.

Initially, I could not find the words to say 'hi' or 'hello' or 'how are you doing?' Instead, I just smiled and fumbled around with the flowers that I had brought. My heart sank so. I did not know what to say. I remember clearly the war of words in my head. 'Ask her how she is'—'Ask about the surgery'— 'Has the cancer gone?'

'Don't be stupid!' another voice retorted. 'You know exactly how she is—she looks terrible! "Has the cancer gone?"!' the other voice mocked me.

I just sat on the windowsill and we exchanged greetings. You looked as if you were in so much pain and my heart ached for you.

I hope you have forgiven the way I was unable to stay. I really hope you have. I don't know if you could see me, but I was trembling so much. I felt surrounded by death. I could see it. I could feel it. I was also aware that any moment I could start crying. And I knew that it would not be silent tears running daintily down my cheeks, tears that I could dab at gently. They would have been uncontrollable sobs and screams of unfairness of it all. They would have been questions, wondering how was it possible that such a vibrant beautiful woman like you had been reduced to someone I could hardly recognize. So I left.

Breathing the grey air of London was unusually refreshing from me. It was as if I was escaping from an emotional prison of sorts. On my way down, I saw a couple crying in the corridor. A young man and woman. She was clinging to him as if it were her last hope as she sobbed into his shoulder; he was looking straight ahead, tears cascading fast and furious. It was weird, because I wanted to stop to say something—or had I just wanted to be nosey? Had someone died? Who? Or had they just received bad news about one of their health? My brain took a picture of that scene and I have never been able to forget it.

The air was refreshing, Alero. I don't know what it is about hospitals—or perhaps it was just that particular cancer ward—that makes the smell of disinfectant smell like death cleaned up.

I felt sad leaving you. I also felt relief; you looked painful. I found a coffee shop nearby, because the thought of going home was not appealing. I needed to cleanse my thoughts and my mind.

As I waited for my tea, my mind strove desperately to stay focused on the present. It was unable to.

Not reluctantly, I was taken back to when we first met. We had hit it off instantly. I thought you were a bit of a drama queen. It was at a friend's granddaughter's naming ceremony. You know what it is like in Nigeria; we have these elaborate ceremonies to name a child. Very cultural and traditional. We were both friends of the grandmother. I was expecting my first child and you were so happy for me. It had taken a long time coming. There was an immediate bond between us. It just goes to show that sometimes you do not need several years of friendship to establish a long, trusting relationship. We spend the most of that day talking as if we were long lost friends. My spirit was definitely in tune with yours!

You hear people say or write that it seemed 'such a long time,' but in actual fact it was so short a time for us between events. We had hardly got to know each other when you were diagnosed with breast cancer. It was an advanced stage. We were all devastated. After that, events took over, as much as our paths were destined to merge together, they were apart.

***

Foster's Story

"Adversity is the inspector of our constitutions; she simply tries our muscle and powers of endurance, and should be a periodical visitor...."

I set the context of my memories with these sombre words from George Meredith in *The Pilgrim's Scrip*, written in 1888. It does not in any way seek to define Alero's life; in fact, she is more that this combative firefighter whose life is chronicled with the monotony of events and adversity—not just one setback but a series of coordinated misfortunes that conspired to stop her from finding happiness and achieving goals. Alero has one of the finest, most logical minds; she is a thoughtful, ambitious woman who put so much into life but has been unjustly robbed by events beyond her control. The focus of this narrative has been to present an overcomer who has developed the rare spirit of triumph to continue life with a great degree of normalcy not found in many cancer survivors. Her joie de vivre remains undiminished.

I met Alero at University of London; we both had passion for the Law and came with rich backgrounds of academic achievement. But the ties that bind our friendship were shaped, strengthened and nurtured by our shared capacity to overcome adversity in a manner which amazed many.

When Alero was diagnosed with cancer, I met her for lunch. With latent feelings of fear, trepidation and exasperation, I told her to be strong because all would be well with her in the end. My words reverberated in my psyche for many weeks, as if I had been disingenuous to a very dear friend in time of her greatest vulnerability. Given the ease with which abundance of good health promotes vivacity and infuses life with deep purpose and meaning, it is incredible how swiftly events like the diagnosis of critical illness can take away those certainties in life which we have often taken for granted.

I began to ask many questions as I trudged along this rough, dark alley of guilt: What power did l have to provide such assurances in such grim situations? Who am I to lift this beacon of hope at this cross road of life and death and maintain such a cheerful front for my friend? I got to know from Alero afterwards that my words had a profound impact on her ability to stay sane and upbeat. This gave me enormous sense of relief and fulfilment.

When it was all over, we met again for a catch up. It was obvious that she was drained from this relentless pursuit of life and calm normality. She took a deep sigh, and then a shocking burst of emotion came out. She said, 'Foster, life is overrated!'

This chilling pathos which those words conveyed will never depart from me. They underscored the enormity of the fight, as if it was a pyrrhic victory—more or less tantamount to a defeat. I disagreed with her vehemently, and still do so now! It was worth the fight and the victory from cancer is resoundingly sweet for all of us who still have Alero with us.

Those of us who have had the privilege to interact with Alero during those turbulent years of chemo, surgeries and side effects, can testify to what her indomitable desire to live and banish despair can achieve. Her tale of untold triumph, courage and shear grit has unfolded in this book.

***